T0245426

I have here dealt with the wall of Taboos which silenced our thoughts, emotions, and aspirations.

I hope my poetry is deeply "interior and personal-which the reader recognizes as his own" as Salvatore Quasimodo once said.

Preface

I've known Paul Zeppelin for almost sixty years since 1961. At first, I met him as a painter. The remarkable thing at the time was that Paul, like no other, developed a special relationship between the hue and the semantics of his paintings. The most ordinary objects, such as a tin can or a burned match, turned on his canvas straight into a dramatic and often tragic story. At least that's how the viewer perceived his pictures and rewarded the painter with fascination and deservedly popularity.

Over the years, Paul Zeppelin developed his art into ever broader genres. Thus, his relationship found in painting between the elemental (hue) and complex (meaning, subject, meaning) was transformed into the relationship between the tone and the statement in his poems, which Paul wrote in recent years in English.

So now the musical, the tone has taken on the role of the former hue, and the sound lately made sense. The power of this poetic collection is a seamlessly interwoven fabric of sound and meaning that leads us into the world of faith and doubt, of peace and war, of death and life, despair and hope...

Zeppelin's poems must be heard from the first row and then read by the eyes.

Boris Schapiro

Boris Schapiro is the author of "Соло на флейте", "Metamorphosenkorn", "Ein Tropfen Wort", "Aufgezeichnete Transzendenz", and 21 other literary works in German and Russian.

Dawn Poured Its Rays into My Room

I watched my nightly dreams in gray;
Dawn poured its rays into my room,
I grabbed my always ready broom
And quickly swept them right away.

I wished to find in the darkness,
Not in the blinding light,
The truth which rarely sparkles
Under the starless night.

However, in the morning of a day,
When coffee is the eloquence of life,
When daring winds are on the way,
I seek a pearl of wisdom in my strife.

My soul is coldly soaked.
I raised my trembling voice
In the hostile, piercing rain.
The trees are still uncloaked,
I really had no other choice,
But funnel life into the drain.

I try to find a panacea for this rust,
While life acts like a stubborn horse
Without a saddle, spurs and reins;
I live in mediocrity, inhale the dust;
I hardly breathe, my anger soars,
And clogs my dog-tired veins.

Like bees in search of fitting hives,
I'm discovering the arteries of lives.

I Need a Pair of Wings

I need a pair of wings
Burned with the sun,
I play the strings,
My fingers run,
I spur my horse,
Along my verse.

Nobody sings
The songs I wrote;
I need a pair of wings
To keep my poetry afloat.

I'd like to know:
Am I a chicken or a hen?
What if I am a nasty crow?
Who cares, we're old friends,
I didn't notice who went first
Into the dreadful lions' den
To shake few friendly hands,
To see whose bubbles burst.

I want to dance with you,
I would prefer in heaven,
The bird of hope is blue,
I am an old black raven.

The Night Has Opened Its Umbrella

The night has opened its umbrella.
Bright stars swam in my wine,
And Elgar's Opus 85 for cello
Embraced this weary soul of mine.

The bed was awfully cold without you;
The wind was softly singing lullabies,
The rain drummed something blue,
I tried, but couldn't close my eyes.

I tried to live with hope and love;
I used to hide my pains and fears,
Even my angel-savior far above
Missed warnings of those years.

Old willows wept with silver leaves,
The days were clouded by griefs.
The starry nights were long and dark
Reflected in the river of my tears.
You walked away and took my heart,
Despair descended on my cheers.

The blade of lightning parts the sky,
Long narrow shadows scar the wall,
I'm ready to unfurl my wings and fly,
I'm sure, my saints won't let me fall.

We are just actors on the stage.
We fade away and leave no trace,
When times rewrite our final page.
Our virtuous sins will melt in grace.

The night has opened its umbrella,
Bright stars swam into my wine,
And Elgar's Opus 85 for cello
Embraced this weary soul of mine.

3

Empty Pages

I spoon-fed timid yesterdays,
I kicked the can down the road,
I didn't know any better ways
To be noticed or to be heard.

I'm reading these tea leaves,
And see a pile of shattered hopes,
I see a bunch of smirking thieves
Cheating their chairs and ropes.

I hear the Devil's monologue,
And stand in aweless silence,
I cannot fight this demagogue,
I need my angels' guidance.
As always, they are far above,
They hardly ever guide or love.

Life built for us few stages,
We are the actors, having fun.
There's nothing new under the sun,
Unless we leave our golden cages.

What's gone must yet return
At dawn, before the midday burn.
Life-theatre is for those who yearn
To walk against the winds
Filled with the voices of the past,
Against the winds that howl,
But never throw in the towel.

A meek and colorless routine-
New garbage in, old garbage out-
A timeworn never-ending scene.
Nothing to write back home about,
Only the tiny incremental changes
Cast shadows on my empty pages.

I Carved My Rosy Dreams

I am confused,
My literary wins are punished;
I am amused,
My literary sins are varnished.

At times, I am a snake,
At times, I am a hawk,
At times, I give or take,
At times, I run or walk.
At night, all cats are gray,
It is the price we have to pay.

Life is my prey no more,
I'll return to its offended heart;
I am a sailor come ashore
That promised never to depart.

I watch my dreams at night,
I pen ten inches every day;
At dusk, life serves a tray
With my excruciating pain,
Left by an avalanche of joy,
Lit by a blinding candlelight.
At dawn, I vigorously feign
That I am a poet, not a decoy.

A splendid god Apollo said:
"A poem is a living object,
A language manipulating
Sounds irrelevant to truth.
Only fresh verses soothe
The thirst of futile waiting
Without common sense,
Without reasons or ideas."

I carved my rosy dreams
Across a fluffy rug of snow,
Along the feisty streams
Enjoying their eternal flow.

I Cast My Nets upon the World

The medals earned
With dullness of a sword,
The lessons learned
With sharpness of a word.

I can't forget that deck
Of playing cards;
I can't forget that wreck
Of our noble goals.
I can't forgive the reigns
Of merciless hearts;
I can't forgive the pains
Of shattered souls.

I am a fisherman of dreams,
I cast my nets upon the world;
I sail my milk and honey streams,
I am your captain," All aboard"!

My sails unfurled,
Streams run along the trees
Toward the Third,
The Holy Ghost above the seas.

I didn't see the other Two
After I met the Ghost,
I missed that rendezvous,
I couldn't leave my outpost.

Winged Pegasus, dear horse,
I ride you in my lonely nights,
Above the interwoven vines
Where stars review my verse.
They share divinity of lights,
They read between my lines.

Cherchez La Femme

Old calendars make our days immortal,
Although, the angered winds of autumn,
Without any shame strip bending trees,
And watch the dance of swirling leaves.

Leaves fall and help to write this epigram,
I hear their whisper, "Cherchez la femme."
It sounds like a murmur of an old coquette,
I'm asked to search for someone to forget.

I'm standing on the Pont des Arts, at noon,
Over the tides forgotten by the lazy moon.
The wicked weather seduces naked trees.
If this is not a promised paradise, what is?

Bacchanalia

Fat Bacchus looked me in the eyes,
His jolly face was kind and ruby red,
The wine he poured deserved a prize,
He was entirely naked -not a shred.

There were some dancing girls,
Nude, cute, no shoes, no pearls,
Plenty of music, food and wine,
No wonder, Bacchus was divine.

His band was playing drums and flutes,
I sensed no rhythm among those suits,
I guess they were delivered by a stork,
They ate and drank, but never worked.

Those little cupids, Venus' naughty boys,
Brought me a young mermaid, a treasure,
She was so stunning; I even lost my voice,
Even her tail predicted too much pleasure.

I noticed Bacchus came alive and waved,
After a bunch of drinks, I was quite brave,
"Do you prefer to be a mortal or a god?"
He diplomatically answered with a nod.

I liked those Gods, who ate and drank a lot,
Zeus, Bacchus, Neptune or a mortal Lot.
Sometimes, I too was drinking like a fish,
And gladly satisfied my every whim or wish.

Mythology called Bacchus' feasts orgiastic;
At least, this one was utterly bombastic.
I was brought up to trace the wills of gods,
I even gulped from barrels to beat the odds.

Bartender, pour for me another glass,
I will proclaim again, "In Vino Veritas!"

I Brought Her a Bouquet

I had a life the other day,
I had a wife, but yesterday.

I brought her a bouquet
Of wilted roses
And left them at the door
With love in tender petals.
I wrote a little note:
"Forget your normal nay,
Forget your futile poses,
It's worth much more
Than all the other gifts
Of precious metals."

The dog-eared pages
Of my tattered days,
Like older tired actors
Who left their stages,
Like my unpublished
Chapters,
Won't see my fame's
Alluring rays.

That time has finally
Arrived,
When no one grades
My papers.
I failed before I thrived;
Above the slums I saw
Skyscrapers,
Surrounded by maples
To entertain their souls
With leafy benedictions,
And lead our tired eyes

To underground cables
Buried in narrow holes,
With our subscriptions
To electronic paradises.

I had a life the other day,
I had a wife but yesterday.

Another Trojan Horse

Another Trojan horse
Is waiting on my lawn,
Today I'm not naïve, of course,
The Greeks have never gone.

Her velvety appearance,
A silent echo of the past,
A useless perseverance,
An olden mold, but finer cast.

Attractive as unexpected money,
Despite the warriors concealed.
She looks like an Easter bunny,
Left in the middle of a battlefield.

There is no anger anymore,
People are people; war is war.
My lost naiveté is only theft,
There's nothing of real value left.

The last still-hanging leaf
Won't ask about its tomorrow,
Life is too brief
To dwell on yet another sorrow.

Another Trojan horse
Stands on my lawn,
I lock the doors;
Life's going on.

Artful Uncertainty

The grass is greener past the fence,
No one has time to count chickens yet,
Fall is a time for picky mating hens
And every rooster gets a Russian nyet.

We like the nights of nonconformity,
We hate the days of social correctness,
We long for lives of artful uncertainty,
Self-reassured and arrogantly reckless.

Our yesterday still sings,
"When we were kings..."
But history doesn't repeat itself,
It's rather turning on a dime.
We wouldn't keep it on a dusty shelf,
We would rewrite its fragile paradigm.

We comb haystacks for hidden needles,
For bits of secrets sowed by our gods,
For the ideas of intellectual diehards.
We crave the eyes of mighty eagles
To see the truth beyond facades
Of non-existing houses of cards.

A pitiless mentality and vicious styles
Of games around bright green tables
Created men living as solitary isles,
As modern heroes of ancient fables.

The saints unfurled their wings
And tried to navigate our souls;
The fallen angel pulled the strings
And we rewrote the Dead Sea scrolls.

A Dungeon for Imperfect Lives

My never-ending quietism
Led me to the nickname dreamer,
And to old-fashioned symbolism
Squeezed out by a poetic reamer.

The devil feeds me from a trough,
I cannot live in this quagmire,
I take my velvet kid gloves off,
And hold his hoofed feet to the fire.

I know of a den for fallen angels,
A dungeon for imperfect lives
With a few chairs for strangers
And for the true believers' lies.
I'd like to stop there for a day
As Jesus did on the way to bliss.
I wonder if He misses the abyss,
While managing the Milky Way.

It is about six o'clock,
It is my morning walk.
A totally indecent rising sun,
Too fast, elite, and avant-garde
As if it wants to outrun
Its underground nightly guard.

I am still skating on the razor
Between sunrises and sunsets;
Never as a bourgeois stargazer,
But as a bard of social upsets.

I Often Pray in Empty Chapels

I touched
The cooler side of pillows,
I learned
The darker side of souls,
I walked
The shady side of streets
Under the weeping willows,
I knew
Futility of fearless roles
In front of empty seats.

I envy my own place
In this absurdly complex space,
Protected from a dire calamity,
Enjoying vulgar commonality
Of daily pseudo-scientific lies
Devouring our lifeless lives.

I asked,
"What price one pays
To live in the insanity of days?
Which war one fights
To live in the duality of nights?
How much one has to owe
To live banalities of daily flow?
To live finalities of status quo?"

My questions fell on idle ears,
I was encircled with my peers.
Looking for low hanging apples.

I often pray in empty chapels.

Her Life's Dried Out Riverbeds

We can't return into the past,
The future is a dire nightmare,
As long as chilly winters last,
We drown in their murky glare.

We watch the stripes of light
On our mother's loving face,
The day is young and bright
Beyond our Venetian shades.

We see, I and my brother,
Her long hair silver threads,
The wrinkles of our mother,
Her life's dried out riverbeds.

Our strategies and tactics,
Our counselors and friends,
Even our clever witty antics
Can't flood these riverbeds.

The salty rivers of her tears
Run into the sea of sorrows,
The arid desert of her years
Scorch our cold tomorrows.

Don't elongate our rope,
Take our dreams away,
We slide down the slope,
The skies above still gray.

Dark Angel is already here,
We face his piercing stare,
The drums of war are near,
The lies are marching bare.

We went into the alien Hell,
We fought for gloomy goals,
Nobody heard our farewell,
They saw our soaring souls.

We saw, I and my brother,
Two brave and loving lads,
The wrinkles of our mother,
Her life's flooded riverbeds.

I Breathe the Air of Glee

Take me to your home,
Don't send me to my past;
Give me a tiny ray of light,
Don't ask where I am from,
I know I am not the last
To be with you this night.

A working girl,
A loving heart,
A shiny pearl,
A piece of art.

I love; therefore, I live,
The angels take, you give.
You are my morning dew,
I am a captive loving you.
Don't ever set me free,
I breathe the air of glee.

Homage to Eugene Ionesco

A glass of brandy
Resting in his hand;
Another miserable day,
But he is fine and dandy.
His head is in the sand,
Not yet on the Herod's tray.

He is neither a red meat
Nor fowl,
He is not a damp fruitarian
Salami,
He is a wolf, who cannot
Howl,
He is an ice-covered ocean
Near Miami.

He has a fruitless wish,
He teaches his goldfish
To walk, to talk and cry,
Although the bowl is dry.

As futile as the broken scissors
He can no longer sail his ship;
Nether his gods nor Caesars
Shelter his dead-end trip.

His calls of the absurd
No one can understand,
He's a hovering bluebird;
Inferno is his wonderland.

He smiled from ear-to-ear,
When critics lost the flow.
He knew that death is near
For his off-Broadway show.

A glass of brandy
Rested in his hand,
Another miserable day,
But he was fine and dandy,
His head was in the sand,
Not yet on the Herod's tray.

Homage to D. M. Thomas

Alone, therefore I am wild
Frustrated naughty ox,
I am as candid as a child,
Shrewd as a golden fox.

I love you only,
I am still naïve,
I am still lonely,
I am free to grieve.

I live in depth of silence,
Converse in lowest tones,
No passion - only science,
Only my soul still mourns.

Youth is a lavish lender,
Smart, kind and tender,
A sinless angel of salvation,
A beacon of transfiguration.

I walked into the scene
Of a forgotten love intrigue
That's hard to comprehend;
Demanding and obscene,
I leaped into a weird fatigue
To camouflage that trend.

My mortal sins
Will be dissolved
Or washed away,
Life always wins;
I lived and loved,
I didn't miss a day.

I am a fallen raven,
I am a slave of love,
Yet bold, not craven,
I never have enough.

Homage to Beethoven

The concertmaster brotherly veers
Well starched white tied magicians,
Their shiny toys and perfect ears
Serve loyally the trained musicians.

A baton-lightning is swiftly raised,
Despotic as a commanding sword,
The notes are lovingly embraced
And thrown into this patient world.

First violins' nocturnal whispers
Lift weightless brilliance of halos
Above the lowest octaves-sisters
From velvety, but bossy cellos.

The piano came to grab the stage,
The cymbals pierced our defenses,
Amid conductor's well staged rage
I heard the strings of gentle senses.

A loud silence of the last accord,
The final opulence of culmination.
Ludwig Beethoven gave his Lord
The hallowed fruit of admiration.

Homage to Perlman

This night I have returned,
The sky of Italy was burned.
I heard a god. I won't forget
The firebird of that last sunset.

Guarneri, Stradivari or Amati
Soared to their music's grace
Crisp like the sweet biscotti
Under the amaretto glaze.

The great cathedral of Cremona;
The nave is packed with people;
The air reminds me of a sauna;
The sounds rock on every ripple.

Divine Itzhak is on the stage,
Plays Paganini's number one:
The gentle filigree of outrage,
Celestial acrobatics of a strife.

Long after Perlman has gone
I hear the grandeur of his life.

Homage to Japan

The heaven's manna
Of creative powers,
The harmony of Ikebana,
The elegance of flowers.

The waltz of crispy snow,
The quiet soothing bliss,
Sun melts the silky throw
Under the midget trees.

I like Japan without pardons
With formal dinners on the floor,
With grace of the ancient culture,
With those minimalistic gardens,
With gorgeous geishas at the door
Wiping their tears at my departure.

She made for me a paper crane,
She put it gently in my hand;
The merciless steam of our train
Forever stole me from my friend.

Fast trains of life pass tiny stations
As if competing with a daily breeze.
Those enigmatic rituals of geishas,
Exotic wisdoms of their misty tease.

Homage to Thieves and Whores

I'm fighting tooth and nail
With pencil pushing powerholders
For the freedom to succeed or fail
Under the burden on my shoulders.
I'm not a beast; I'm not a bird,
But I'm a bird among the beasts.
The Holy Trinity retains me as a third.
I am the ghost; I am deceased.

I soar above the stinking seas of lies,
Flanked by my abandoned dreams
Descending from the crying skies
And blinking like confetti in sunbeams,
Landing on busy brides and grooms,
Landing on brittle peace and ugly wars,
Landing on gloomy graves and tombs,
Landing on happy thieves and whores.

We steadily becoming whores or thieves,
Two cornerstones of great civilizations,
New Adams and new Eves
Of great and self-respecting nations.
They're the saints and sinners,
They're the alphas and omegas,
They're the losers and the winners,
They're the silage of Las Vegas.
Life doesn't like a simple story
Of innocence and opened doors,
Life rests on wilted laurels of its glory,
Fringed by the thieves and whores.

Here's my confession and remorse,
What's in the name?
Amid the girls, I choose the whores,

The diamonds we so unfairly blame.
Occasionally, I choose the thieves,
The precious fallen golden leaves.
My colleagues from the Holy trinity
Take all the sinners to infinity.

I'm Leaving Earth

We try to flee and rest,
We let all worries fade away,
Our journey is a quest
For breathing yet another day.

While in the saddles
We count wins and losses,
Some get gold medals,
Some, only boneyard crosses.

Life is a spectacle for haters,
The show of a slaughterhouse,
Our jaded modern gladiators
Enjoy a game of cat and mouse.

I saw their motto on the wall,
Daring calligraphy in chalk,
It said, "Life is a shopping mall."
I ran away- no time to walk.
.

Too ignorant and shameless,
They are already lost at birth,
They're happy being brainless,
I'm sorry, but I'm leaving Earth.

I Cannot Play a Second Violin

Don't stare at me
With reprimanding eyes,
I haven't lost the key
From the packed paradise.

I tried to wake a sleeping tiger,
I gave an eagle flying lessons,
I daringly ignored a clicking Geiger,
Life never hid from me its essence.

I outfoxed the holy inquisition,
I confidently jumped the bail,
I didn't waste my ammunition,
I simply pulled my fortune's tail.

I cannot play a second violin,
I thrust through thick and thin,
I like to steer a ship from time to time,
I like to get a grip on pious paradigm.

The dazzling sensuous tonalities
Of Stradivarius' faultless violins,
The obvious and frivolous banalities
Of our seven uninspiring mortal sins.
Don't baffle or confuse me anymore,
I am a self-righteous church's whore.

Don't stare at me
With reprimanding eyes,
I haven't lost the key
From the required paradise.

I Hold the End of a Rope

I hold the end of a rope,
My thoughts are clear,
I fear without hope,
I hope without fear.

My idle days lost vigor,
I climb the wall of worry,
The world looks bigger
From the second story.

I hear a covered lie
In every spoken word,
I wonder when and why
Our ethics left the world.

I often hear the voices
Of demons in disguise,
They rudely strip me
Of my sacred choices:
They steal my glee,
They leave my cries.

I gulped a shot of whisky
And gave an olive branch
To my reflection
In the mirror.
At night, I see my days
Much clearer.

My dog still barks
At swirling sparks
Above the briar,
Farewell, bonfire.
My heart is cold,
It's time to fold.

I Need a Shrink

The sun is climbing in the sky,
A jumpy breeze slaps lazy sails
And rocks my stubborn boat.
The hungry seagulls tensely fly,
While all the pirates' fairytales
Advising me to stay afloat.
Life flows like a nervous river,
Whether I am a taker or a giver,
Depending on the banknotes
And portraits on the other side.
I am stuck among the towboats
Rocking my nightmares on a tide.

Life serves me TV dinners,
I share them with the saints,
I am the worst among the sinners,
Even my angel looks and faints.
The fans of a subservient idolatry
May like these half-baked meals,
Just keep their egos a tad burned.
I tossed away my training wheels,
My life is clearly better unadorned.

Tonight, I caught bartender's eyes
And said, "Get me a bigger glass,
Pour me an awkward hefty drink
From mixed vulgarities with class
Over a few rocks of ice."
He coolly said, "You need a shrink."

The words unsaid, the songs unsung,
My disillusionment was not yet wept;
The night was calm and young;
My guilty conscience peacefully slept.

I won't return into my sorrows,
I can no longer bear my past,
I crave my eloquent tomorrows,
I long for happy days that last.

Ode to Love

I'll dress my bride in hugs and kisses.
I'll turn her joyful teardrop into a pearl.
She is so gorgeous and delicious,
I can't imagine any other girl.

The saints are watching from above,
The birds are singing with obsession,
White bells of lilies ring our tune of love
As innocently sensitive as a confession.

White little birch, please, be my bride;
Don't read a textbook's dated pages,
Let's find our promised land. I'll guide.
We'll love and wander through the ages.

Ode to Nice

Waves spanking mercilessly the shiny rocks
And hungry seagulls make odd angry noises,
The rainbow of umbrellas paints ladies' locks,
Quick waiters hustle drinks towards our voices.
I see a few delicious, topless girls,
I like these cute Riviera's pearls
Caressed by a gentle salty breeze;
I am so happy ...I'm in Nice!
The Holy Trinity, a jewel of the Russian churches,
Musée Chagall surrounded with tender birches,
Boulevard Victor Hugo flanked with plane trees;
I am so happy ...I'm in Nice!
A walk along the Promenade cures all my ills,
The Old city's streets stream from the hills,
Between Cafe Turin and Musée Matisse;
I am so happy...I'm in Nice!
The opulent Hotel's "Negresco" art Nouveau,
Its overbearing style preserves the status quo,
The ceilings painted with the scenes of bliss;
I am so happy...I'm in Nice!
A Maître D himself brought my Champagne,
After a wrinkled fifty, he knew I was insane'
He vanished after an accented "pardon, please";
I am so happy...I'm in Nice!
The young concierge offered a "room with air",
Then led me to the terrace and pulled a chair,
Then placed a Damask napkin onto my knees;
I am so happy...I'm in Nice!

The sun descends around five o'clock,
The pompous yachts glide into the dock,
Cheerful tourists look like walking geese;
I am so happy...I'm in Nice!

I order my beloved Soup de Poisson,
The waiter asks me not to call him un garcon,
He said, "I'm a man without tips and extra fees":
I am so happy...I'm in Nice!
While ladies say "fromage" and take their photos,
I look at their well-grown and long-legged daughters.
In vain, I pose like an ancient acrobat on his trapeze;
I am so happy...I'm in Nice!
My hair is gray, I live and spend my pennies.
Sometimes I feel like Thomas Mann in Venice.
Like an old and spiky dinosaur before the freeze;
I'm still happy...I'm still in Nice!
The capital of decadence, here is my premise:
The greatest book I've read is *Death in Venice*,
I'll write my own and name it *Death in Nice*;
Meanwhile, I'm happy and alive. I live in Nice.

I Missed the Fork

Speak, if I am wrong,
I bought it for a song:
Life's hasty as a wink,
At times, I miss a dawn;
Life isn't what you think,
Life's what you've done.

I tasted sounds,
I heard the tastes,
Within the bounds
Of worthless waste.

I missed the fork
And hit the tree,
I am in the morgue,
I am dead but free.

It's not so bad,
I finally am free,
I fetched my glee;
I finally am dead,
And never breathe,
I earned my wreath.

My widowed wife
Flies on the broom;
She needs a life,
She needs a groom.

I Miss the French Riviera and Provence

I miss the French Riviera and Provence,
Those foamy tides and whispers of the sand,
My Cote d'Azur, I fell in love with you at once,
I always dream of you, you're my wonderland.

Four giants-artists dwelling in my heart,
Cezanne, Chagall, Picasso and Matisse
Revealed the naked truth of modern art
When Mother Nature danced striptease.

I miss the food and wines of Luberon,
The Abby's lavender and silver olive trees,
Red sandy hills and rocks of Roussillon,
Flirtatious promenade of charming Nice,
The yachts of Monaco in a gentle breeze,
The walnut leaves around cheese Banon,
A dark mistral above the harbor of Cassis,
The stoic Chateauneuf du Pope in Avignon,
The fiery bulls of Arles that stomp the ground;
A cheval blanc is galloping across Camargue;
A choo-choo train is ready for another round,
Reminds me of a living thing from Noah's ark;
The films in Cannes and glamour of two weeks,
Nude beaches and some newer risqué trends,
L'isle-sur-la-Sourge with bridges and antiques,
I miss my bosom hilly friend St-Paul-de-Vence.
I miss those curly narrow climbing streets of Eze,
The weary harbor of Marseilles with bouillabaisse,
Old Montpelier with tatty manuscripts menagerie,
A quiet Robion where strangers call you Mon Ami.

I miss flamboyant years of Saint-Tropez,
A grandiose arcade of Pont du Gard,
Bandol's refreshing stream of a cold Rose,

The five o'clock Pastis of Paul Picard.
I miss the elegance and glory of Antibes
Still nothing short of lustrous,
Perfumes of Grasse, nobody dares to crib
That hover above ceramics of the masters.

To you, blue waters of the sea
Caressing lazy sunny beaches,
To you, my Cote d'Azur, I say merci
Without boring, pompous speeches.

I miss the French Riviera and Provence,
A blinding paradise, I fell in love at once.

I Miss the Heat

I rubbed the sparkly lamp,
I found the Aladdin's gold,
Behind the highway ramp,
I didn't pick it up--too cold.

Forget the spring,
The winter rolls,
The snow falls
On our street.

I miss the heat;
And throw my hat
Into the ring:
I sip Jack Daniels and sing
About hating winter's threat,
And think about sunny rays,
And play my whiny old guitar,
And hop the calendar of days
Towards the spring; it isn't far.

I found the Aladdin's gold;
I didn't pick it up--too cold.

I Miss You, Abigail

We didn't need a Holy cross,
Our fates were tightly willed,
It was our tragedy and loss,
Our happiness was killed.

I miss your cheerful blue eyes,
Their sea of godsend lightness,
Your graciously ironic smiles,
Your generosity and brightness.

I walked, I sailed, I flew,
I looked for one like you,
Your replicas were pale,
I miss you, Abigail.

I've read your laughter,
I didn't need the Braille,
I knew what I was after,
I miss you, Abigail.

So elegant and never loud,
So captivating in any crowd,
You are a singing nightingale,
I miss you, Abigail.

You were a jewel, a treasure,
A diamond of every pleasure,
You left behind a happy trail,
I miss you, Abigail.

Without you, I am so frail,
I am a boat that lost its sail,
You were my Holy Grail,
I miss you, Abigail.

I Love My Solitude

The memories are tough
On my nostalgic tray;
My well-arranged bouquets
Like diamonds in the rough,
Won't bring a dissent day
For our disappearing love.

I walk over a wrinkled lake,
Across the frozen ripples,
And lean against the wind;
I wish I had a magic rake
To gather all the peoples
Who lived yet never sinned.

I don't ride horses in the field,
I wrestle with my broken chair.
I never rush ahead, I yield,
I have no passionate affair.

I am wrapped in truth,
But stuffed with lies;
The former fits my youth,
The latter fits the vice.

Don't rush to say goodbye,
Wait for my ascending sigh;
I try, but can't decide it now,
Why do I have to buy a cow
If I am gulping her milk free?
I'd like to drown in this glee.

I am still homeless,
I didn't change my attitude:
At times, I love aloneness,
Tonight, I love my solitude.

I Love the Movies of Tomorrow

I tried, but failed to hide disdain
For cheesy movies of the past:
Somebody dances in the rain,
Somebody climbs a broken mast,
Somebody asks to play again,
Somebody doesn't give a damn,
Somebody has a holiday in Rome,
Somebody builds St. Peter's dome,
Somebody craves her early fame,
Somebody builds the Notre Dame,
Somebody tries to catch a thief,
Somebody says it's all about Eve.

I hate the movies of today:
Somebody hides that he's gay
Somebody mourns, but kills,
Somebody prays, but steals,
Somebody fights the navy seals,
Somebody forges ancient wills,
Somebody burns the books,
Somebody robs the homeless,
Somebody catches filthy crooks,
Somebody was unjustly hacked,
Somebody feels totally I helpless.

I think the ship of fools is wrecked.
I love the movies of tomorrow,
We lend, the bankers borrow…

I Built a House from a Dream

I built my house from a dream.
The sun is smiling on the floor,
You slowly walk and gleam,
Our happiness waits at the door.

Our first tender dates
Sunk into the tight embraces;
Two lives, two fates;
A selfie with two happy faces.

To you, my love, I bring
A bird of bliss in hand,
Into the rite of spring,
Into our wonderland.

The petals of white flowers
Cover your tender shoulders,
A gorgeous shawl for hours
Of our first nightly wonders.

A fragile light,
A jolly laughter,
A lovely sight;
A morning after.
We are together,
Two wedding rings,
Birds of a feather,
Each flies and sings.
The wars were fought,
The scars were earned.
Loves were not taught,
Loves were not learned.

The trail of love is dry:
Our happiness delayed;
We didn't fail to try,
We tried and failed.
A drop of rain, the sky is clear,
It is your pain; it is my only tear.

I built my house from a dream,
The sun is crying on the floor,
Life lost its tempting gleam.
I am alone; I locked the door.

I Loved My Nanny

I'm quietly and aimlessly strolling within my past:
I like the pleasant fog of my nostalgic labyrinths;
I paved my tiny path to this maniacal indulgence.
I see my nanny breast-feeding a homeless guy,
I always valued her magnanimous selflessness.
The dome of innocent cathedral of my tired soul
Hosting the clouds shaped like wingless angels,
Noiselessly wandering along the white columns
And the rays of sun gently caressing their faces.
These mirages last longer than influential reality
Which wears a rusty chastity belt. I have the key.
The truth is vulnerable, the lies are impenetrable.
I sense the nervousness in expectancy of grace,
The quiet breeze of premonition is not a tailwind,
I clinch my teeth and plow ahead along my smile.
Grace under pressure is the virtue of phoniness.
Two halves of my intellect unexpectedly collided
As loud cymbals in a marching band of wartime.
The Big Bang, Bagdad, a bag lady of a bad Dad.
I have a craving for writing; some think it is a gift,
I'm reading my morbid fables between the lines,
I cannot read; therefore, my tales stay seamless.
Wagner's music embraces visitors of Auschwitz.
I can no longer bear the pain of God's mistakes.
I loved my nanny; long live my visits to the past!

I Left the Tower of Despair.

The bank was local, small;
I watchfully went inside,
A camera on every wall,
No cops or guards in sight.

A young and friendly clerk
Asked if she could help me,
I didn't want to be a jerk,
"Give me the money!
One, two, three..."

In disbelief she smirked
And grabbed my firearm.
Another anxious, nasty clerk
Found a knob of the alarm.

Four cops hurried inside;
I didn't steal a single dime.
They cuffed me on the site
And solved "a perfect crime".

I never went to jail:
I watched it in a film,
I jumped the bail.
I sailed to Cuba, faraway,
And took a loud pseudonym
Of Papa Hemingway.

I drank, but wrote good novels.
I earned great fame and wealth,
I couldn't write anything else,
I pulled a gun and shot myself.

Why didn't I hide from spooks
Under the name of Homer;

I would be blind, but sober,
And write only two books.

Too late, I gulped my bottle,
I couldn't take it anymore.
It was my fate. I lost a battle,
But sadly, won the futile war.

I Left a Bitter Message

I left a bitter message
On my annoying phone,
A boneyard for wreckage
Of our egos carved in stone.

My beer was dark,
I slurped the foam,
I overshot my mark,
It's time to go home.

Another fruitless night,
Died in a tempting light.
I am tired, I cannot write,
My page is snow-white.

It was the longest strife,
I am laden with a verse,
I need a skilled midwife
Instead of a lazy nurse.

Headwinds can't stop me,
I'm veering up and down,
Tailwinds won't help me
In my imaginative flight;
Whether I soar or drown,
I strive to win the fight.

I Live in My Tomorrow

I live, therefore I gamble
Persuaded by my greed,
I am a stranger in a maze,
Continually drift or ramble,
Repetitively lie or plead
Confronted face-to-face.

I keep life for a fool,
They think I am a lifer,
My day is not a school,
But an enigma to decipher.

Mirror, mirror on the wall,
Reveal my seven sins,
Reveal the seven seals,
Reveal the seven dwarfs,
Reveal my seven wins
In seven fruitless wars,
Reveal if I will ever fly,
Reveal if I will ever fall
Or live and never die.

I have a terrible addiction,
I live today in my tomorrow,
I had no life, it was a fiction,
If there is no past, I'll borrow.

I Hope to Be Around for A While

I hope to be around for a while,
I've seen wars, peace and hunger,
I didn't come from the "above",
My life came from the "under".

When we betray ourselves,
We call it reason.
When we betray the others
They call it treason.

Those butchers threw a blanket on my head
To kill my thoughts and mute my voice;
Enough isn't enough; the sky was bloody red,
The life I lived before was not my choice.

The sweaters of despair no one is weaving,
My mother said, "Wait for a sunny day,
Our yesterdays were hardly worth the living,
Our tomorrows aren't far away."

I used to think quite clearly in my youth,
Far back, I knew a lot, but not the truth.

He Slowly Drags his Cart

He knows years of sorrows;
He knows tears of gratitude,
The fears of cold tomorrows,
The quiet cheers of solitude.

He walks lean like a fork;
He calmly drags his cart,
A sad and wingless stork
Carrying the guilt of ours:
A walk of a broken heart,
A funeral without flowers.

There is no place to hide
The stories of a street.
Dark shadow of his dog
Walks by his side
And jumps like a bullfrog
To catch his yummy treat.

Life is a relay's final leg.
Like a goat-legged faun,
He has to play and fight;
He has to bow and beg.
Like a graceful old swan,
Who fades into the night.

A homeless ragged man,
Well charred and seared
With a wine-colored face,
He took my five then ran
And quickly disappeared
Into the downtown maze.

A man who needs to rest,
A gullible, unrealistic child,
He wished us all the best
And strolled into the wild.

Goodbye...

Goodbye,
Sweet love of yesterday,
Goodbye,
My head was on your tray.
Goodbye,
You heard my parting sigh.
Goodbye,
I was a bird without the sky.
Goodbye,
Today, I'm eager to ascend;
Goodbye,
I'll spread my wings and fly.
Goodbye,
It's the beginning of the end,
Goodbye,
No one will ever hear my cry.
Goodbye,
I fought to win my freedom,
Goodbye,
Hello, my precious kingdom.

Forgive me, Mom and Dad

The wombs of dreams,
The embryos of hopes,
The cries and screams
Wait in their envelopes.
Forgive me, Mom and Dad,
I kissed goodbye my youth,
I shall return alive or dead;
This is my brutal truth.

I'm going far away
As one of the few and proud;
The foggy dreams will sway
Above the sea of doubt,
Above the bloody futile wars,
Above the shattered peace,
While our warmongers-whores
Wait for the hell to freeze.

Short days still hide my fears,
I vigorously fight this war;
Long nights will see your tears;
Farewell, I won't be back,
I wish you all the best;
Please, lock the door,
Be blessed..

My Life Abruptly Changed

They say, "You never worked a day
If you enjoyed what you've been doing."
Long live my vanity and pride,
Life was a sinful yet joyous ride.

The angels' fury was unfair,
My life abruptly changed
Without changing masks 'n shrouds;
I noticed that my days and nights
Began their tumbling through the air,
Into the clamor of merciless crowds.

And vanished in the dungeons
Of yet unpublished narcissistic memoirs,
That veer across the labyrinths
Of my perpetual doubts,
Among my clumsy rhymes 'n rhythms,
Besides my ceaseless sways and bouts.

Today, I'm drinking from a fire hose
The choppy waters of my confusions,
I can no longer understand the youth;
Maybe the angels simply put my nose
Into the foggy world of optical illusions,
And I assume that I will see the truth.

Forget the nuts 'n bolts,
The brick 'n mortar,
The tooth 'n nail...
I'm sure, the future holds
And wants to flip a quarter
Which may allow me to win or fail.

I Leave this Bedlam

My fits of melancholy,
My frequent false alarms
Stopped singing holy, holy
And hold me in their arms.

The beauty is diminished,
I try, but cannot pen it well
And fit the melodies of war;
My verse is yet unfinished,
But has returned from hell
And is knocking on my door.

Invite me to a dance,
My hampered madam,
Send off your sorrows,
Fan off your salty tears;
Then I'll take a chance
And leave this bedlam
To entertain tomorrows,
Beyond my tacky years.

I gave away myself
To this unhappy fate;
My life's been strewn
With wars and women;
Fires licked my nights,
And layers of despair
Covered my dull days.

I paged old calendars
Of my lackluster years
And pledged, "As soon

As my setbacks expire,
I will collect a jumble of
My sadly rueful being,
Then I'll triumph over
This unexpected mire."

Forgive Me, Love

Forgive me, Love,
You were a hand,
I was a glove.
You were my friend
You had rose glasses,
You learned the truth
Without taking classes.

So rude, so careless,
I wasn't coy,
You wanted fairness,
But got a sulky boy.

The winter was too close,
My littered, weary soul
Full of sincere remorse
Wrapped in the gold of fall.

Goodbye, my love,
I lost another glove,
The night descended,
Again, I'm empty handed...

I Left My Parachute Behind

My heart and soul are tired,
Enough, I've seen too much,
Even when shots are fired,
I seldom interrupt my lunch.

Long faces shine with lotions,
Long lives wipe bitter tears,
Hard feelings, strong emotions,
No bravery, just sticky fears.

I hiked the labyrinths of words,
Fine-tuning my sclerotic chords.

Talents abandon us in youth,
I wasted many precious pages,
I boldly camouflaged the truth,
I sang of loves without rages.

Today, I am a chosen mourner,
I climb the ecstasy of sadness,
I try to reach the darkest corner
And fall into the pit of badness.

I missed the heavens' stairway,
No one yet knows, I am blind;
I soar across the Milky Way,
I left my parachute behind.

I Listened to the Rain

A premonition of a tender love
Looms like a silhouette of glee,
Sent from the emptiness above
As pointless yet intriguing plea.

After the Big Bang and the Word,
I lived in wilderness of strangers;
Nobody knew our almighty Lord,
No one yet met the fallen angels.

I listened to the rain,
While plowing my life,
And heard: "You're insane,
You try to catch a falling knife,
You run before a moving train".

I knew, red cardinals won't fly
When merciless ravens reign

A magic circle never ends,
It never stops, just bends.
I hear the sabers rattle,
The vultures numbly fly,
Death morphs into a battle,
Life whistles passing by.

Love lingers for another day,
Only farewells remain forever,
Nobody soars above the fray,
No one is that dumb or clever.

Life is hanging on the rope,
River no more, I am a dam,
I wouldn't let my rosy hope
To be a sacramental lamb.

The Night Fell Quickly on the Pond

Late summer. The night fell quickly on the pond,
The weary birds are absolutely quiet,
They want to keep from me their secrets,
Even cicadas seldom scrub their anxious wings.
I sank into the pillows of my rocking chair,
A snifter with cognac gets warm in my palm.

A gentle breeze starts an affair with weeping willows,
I hear their whisper in the silver leaves,
I recognize the words of love,
The branches sway and caress the quiet water
That mirrors endless sky and rocks the winking stars.

My horse is drinking the moon from a gentle pond,
His silhouette is skillfully carved
From the black opal of the night,
His silky tail is idly fanning in the air,
My radio is playing Rachmaninoff's second concerto,
The music is divine ... nirvana.

I finished my cognac,
The nightly tender chill descended on the porch,
I pulled the quilt up toward my chin.
The sneaky shawl of fog crawls through the grass.
A star with a long tail is falling slowly from the sky.
It's a good time to make a wish and close my eyes.

The day is dead,
Long live the day!

Good night.

I Morphed into an Owl

Masts scratch the sky
Above the playful sails,
Old seagulls cry goodbye,
I weep and bite my nails.

I slash with my boat-cleaver
The flows of muddy waters;
A shattered silence of life-river
Sunk memoirs of slaughters.

I wrote the comedies of days
For theaters of the absurd,
I played the tragedies of nights
Between the cheery sunny rays;
I was a wingless, wounded bird,
I longed for happiness of flights.

I waved goodbye
To good-for-nothing days,
And morphed into an owl,
At night, I learned to fly,
Above the silent graves.

The Guillotine of History

The guillotine of history
Beheads the truth,
Obscures the mystery
Of everlasting youth.

Our morality and guilt
Deserve binaural skills
Of decadence and wilt,
Of funerals and thrills.

Unfairness of the day
Descends upon the night,
And all the devils sway
Until the dawn is bright.

We climb the wall of worry,
We fly to reach our goals,
We soar towards the glory,
We play our lifelong roles.

A famous call was made
Before poor Isaac's death,
A faultless twist of fate,
A blind obedience of breath.

When I hear the call,
I'll erase my naughty grin;
When I hear the thunder,
I'll commit my farewell sin.
I'll spiral into a dreadful fall
Toward the fringe of bliss,
Into the silent final blunder,
Into the traitorous abyss.

The guillotine of history
Revealed the mystery
Of God's existence.

A Silver-Washed Moonlight

I soared as Icarus and fell,
I walked the other parallel
Which only imitates realities.
I was a pondering court jester,
I teased such meek banalities,
While a conniving albatross
Settled around his own neck.
These days, I'm a captain
Who anticipates the wreck.

A silver-washed moonlight
Found safe haven on the wall
Above the headboard
Of my squeaky bed,
Viewing emotional affairs
Amid the despair and silence
Of my never-ending visions.

I listened to the whistle blow,
And cheered the rite of spring
Invited by my wintry doubts.
I saw the charming image
Of a spirited scarecrow,
Flaunting her wedding ring
To piercingly invasive crowds.

As an act of faith,
I forever craved
A silver-washed moonlight
That lit the vault of Heaven
Never more frequently
Than every seventh nigh

Eternity for Writers

Nine lives for cats,
Eternity for writers
Killed in the staged combats
Then buried as overnighters.

A woman won't forget;
A man cannot forgive,
Life is a gambling bet:
Some win, some grieve.

My days are hacked
By many tearful goodbyes;
My nights are whacked
By playing games of dice.

I'd like to go back
To change my past
And run the longest track
Along the visions passed.

I've had enough
Of where I've been.
I've had enough
Of what I've missed.
I've had enough
Of what I've seen.
I never had enough
Of whom I kissed.

I'm a thirsty sheep, ram-led,
Inching towards the healing well,
But see the angels wearing red.
I guess it is too late; I am in Hell.

I scream, "My Lord, I am a poet!"
He quietly replies, "I know it."

Our Platoon Marched

The guardian devils soared
Into the blameless skies
Above the killing fields of war,
Like angels in disguise.

A stairway to eternal glory
Was just an ordinary track,
It's better to be safe than sorry,
We couldn't move ahead or back.

We didn't come to leave;
We came to fight and die.
War ran us through a sieve
And hung us mercilessly to dry.
Along the valleys and the hills,
Over the fields of our futile ire,
We simply paid the bills
Of those who sent us to the fire.

My brothers walked an extra mile,
They hoped to reach safe havens;
God hadn't been here in a while,
He left us to the heartless ravens.

Our platoon marched to the sky,
Most never loved or had a drink;
We left behind our farewell sigh;
We stared ahead; we didn't blink.

Few short obituaries with our mugs,
Cold death instead of mothers' hugs,
The soulless men, who sent us here,
Have never fought, just lived in fear.

The power-holders come and go,
Only the memories forever flow.

I Learned to Dream

I learned to dream
When life went up the creek,
I learned to gleam
When life became too meek.

I went to hell to see the glow
And write my darkest prose
About life, cold like the snow
And loveless heart that froze.

At times, life was a predator,
At times, I was its prey,
At times, life was a creditor,
Voiding my wallet every day.

I fought in war that we call life,
I have some scars to verify
That I had losses in this strife;
Yet a few victories and medals,
What I don't flaunt, I am too shy;
I d rather push the other pedals.

I have a sober outlook,
I wouldn't come to Arlington
And lure the fallen to a war;
I've read the Holy Book,
I wouldn't throw the first stone
To hurt a beggar at my door.

Life never was
An all-you-can-eat buffet,
And I am not
Just roaming in the dark;
I am seeking my own way
To leave an earnest mark,
Not a few dollars on a tray.

I am Breaking the Ice

I am breaking the ice,
And rising like a chart
Above the ceiling;
I want to visit paradise
And learn the art
Of the eternal healing.

The thirsty twigs of vines
Parade their ripen treats,
And sip the rainy strings;
Almighty oaks and pines
Flank a few lonely streets
With gentle angel's wings.

I walk the sacred road
Behind my weary soul,
I want my lifelong load
To see the Weeping Wall.

I want to leave the stage
Before the final curtain.
I want to be like you,
I want to leave the cage.
I am absolutely certain,
I want to be a pies Jew.
One of the lucky chosen
For whom Dante's inferno
Remains forever frozen,
But someone always says,
"Buongiorno."

Opium of Fame

I saw timidity and fame,
An unexpected flare;
A sizzling sensual affair
Without praise or blame.

My sleepless night has gone,
And someone said at dawn,
"You aren't just a gifted poet,
You are a great clairvoyant."

A burst of creativity
Requires a total self-denial,
And chocks linguistic relativity;
I have become a lonely isle,
I terminate the boundaries
Between spectacular and vile.

I even purse my lips and blow,
Continuously, but yet in vain,
To calm the sunset's glow
Because I know pain.

I know a doubtless self-love,
I know a devouring romance
Between an actor and a stage;
I never have enough,
I turn to vanity at once,
And lock the golden cage.

I am a frantic troubadour,
I throw logs into the flame,
To see my giant shadow
Extending on the floor.
I taste the opium of fame,
And start a boasting roar
To camouflage my shame.

Homo Homini Lupus Est

The aftershocks of war
Continue to rattle,
Choices defining who we are,
Old soldiers reliving every battle,
Often above or rarely under par.
Their nightmares guide them
Through the years,
Revisiting their sticky fears.

A gory war or a lavish fest,
Stench always hits the fan,
Homo homini lupus est,
A man is a wolf to man.

I've met a celebrated maven,
He taught in Sunday schools;
He didn't give my mind a haven
Among the smart, amid the fools.
He taught about bottom feeders,
He taught to mistrust their words;
He hoped to find better breeders,
I hoped to discover better worlds.

I showed him my empty glass
And asked for an advice or aid;
He never struck a coup de grace,
He knew from what the sausage
Of the gods gets made.

Today, my street is awfully quiet,
Old buddies died. Forever left.
There are no friends to be invited,
I am attached to my nostalgic diet,
Obeying our lives' unending theft-
Our creators were shortsighted.

I Lent my Soul to Badness

I wear the masks of bluff,
I camouflage my sadness,
I laugh, I'm awfully rough;
I lent my soul to badness.

I lost the guiding light,
I wandered in the sky
I plunged into the night
Where dreams don't fly.

I raked my wisdom's morsels,
The sun sent rays into my soul,
I rearranged for you
My life and verses;
Why can't we fly
Before we fall?

The demon's wings
Blocked our sight,
And sent the winds
To stop our flight.

We are two daring cranes,
Let's fly into the isle of hopes
Above the highway lanes,
Above these endless ropes
That kept our hearts at bay.
It's not too late,
Let's celebrate
Our love's delayed birthday.

Graveyards of Hopes

The raging storm of fire
Opened the sacred seal
And learned my old desire,
My secret, my Achilles' hill.

We wear the wedding rings,
Symbols of vanity and pride,
Under the angels' wings
Life flaunts its careless side.

Two lives, two lonely boats,
One sinks, the other floats,
The sadness of blue notes,
Hides in our silent throats.

The truth may set us free,
Lies only postpone the fall,
Just pay the toll
Then stay or flee.

From now it's all downhill,
We burned the slopes,
The time will definitely fill
Graveyards of our hopes.

I Cast Away My Anger

In vain,
I cast away my anger
Politely, like the kings,
And like a plane,
I left the hanger
And spread my wings.

I soared into my dream,
Into the hollow skies
Filled with the gleam
Of our hopes and lies.

I heard the ringing bell
Over the branches' lace;
One of those angels fell
To touch my weary face.

The grace of a fallen angel
Brought glee into my days,
He was a perfect stranger,
He didn't leave a trace...

I Lost My Diamond

I climbed too high
To see her face,
I learned to fly,
But fell from grace.

She had enough,
She wants to love,
She can't forgive,
She can't believe.

I'm a deserted island,
I lost my only love,
I lost my diamond
In the rough.

No one yet knows
When a depression
Ends,
Among the foes?
Among the friends?

I twist myself
Into a pretzel
To understand
The smaller prints.
A pill of Alka Seltzer
Dissolves
My rum's leftovers;
My buddies-rovers
Cheerfully screaming-
I am a pitcher
In the decisive inning.

I Lost a Password

I lost a password
To your heart,
I am overboard,
I am an empty cart.

Unending rain heavily pours,
Eternal pain has no remorse.

Our timeless problems
Nobody yet could solve,
My heart still gambles:
To love or not to love...

I lost a password
To your heart,
Without you I fail;
I am on my knees,
I never had enough,
Forgive me, please.
Only a magic sword,
Only a cherub's dart
May fly to tell the tale
About our ruined love.

We Longed for Glee

Spellbinding tale
Of ancient bards
For every season,
For Hell and paradise,
For sunny days or hale.
Tongue-lashing guards
Kept me in prison,
Lifecycle rolled the dice.

Small town hits the sack,
My prison never sleeps,
The night is scary black,
Farewell escapes my lips

I forged the key,
Unlocked the door,
At last, I am free;
I madly laugh and roar.

My girl conceived the plot,
I knew her classy pedigree,
We quickly tied the knot,
We longed for our glee.

Today, I am on cloud nine,
Today, I am forever free,
My life is spotlessly divine,
Like Eden's Wisdom Tree.

I Look in Silence at the Gold of Foliage

I look in silence at the gold of foliage,
Late autumn holds the end of rope;
I hope to turn my horror into courage,
I wish to morph despair into my hope,
I hope my strength is good enough
To change my rage into a faithful love.

A thin long thread
Of our tormented past
Connecting our lives
To our daily bread,
To those who passed,
To sins of early tribes.

I am walking on eggshells,
Along the poisoned wells
Into a golden mousetrap,
I am ready for my final rap.

Some wrap themselves in sari,
Some disappear into the blue,
The nights are dark and starry
Turn into the sunny days anew,
The grapes which grew in pain
Morph into a great champagne.

I sipped my precious brandy;
The night looks fine and dandy.
Please, come into my world,
It is a joy, just mark my word.

A Crescent Bashfully Hides

I dwelled as a romantic gent,
I played the magic flute of life,
I knew a sweet and sour scent
Of my go-getting deathly strife.

A stream of salty tears
Rolled by my shaggy cheeks
Back to the troubled years
Of endless days and weeks
Among my passionate illusions,
Among my timid and prosaic lies,
Among those worthless fusions
Of quiet triumphs and loud dives.

I innocently struggled in my flights
Over the fate's evasive treasure,
Across my gaudy critical insights,
Along the outbursts of pleasure.

There is a nest in our souls
For imminent departure
Of broken hopes and goals
Into the fertile quiet pasture.

I am a remaining child
Of our last romantic age,
The silver era of the wild
Died out as a weary sage.

A crescent bashfully hides,
A mirror-river floats below,
The stars are basking on
The tides,
And sharing with the night
Their precious glow.

I Loaned my Loneliness to Others

The story is too weird,
It happened just an hour before
The magic disappeared
In premonition of a bloody war,
When reasons lose their battle,
Before the war drums rattle.

A dozen-for-a-dime
The fish begin to rot
From heads downwards,
Life wastes its time,
Life wastes its words
On Mars' audacious plot.

It's like a rearview mirror blur,
A gloomy window to my past,
No one remembers holy myrrh,
Yet gilts of Melchior still last.

Today, I raised my hand
And swore to tell the truth.
I lied, but freed my friend,
I saved veracity of youth.

I'm free, like flow of a waterfall,
I have the right to tell them all
What they don't want to hear.
They cry, I smile from ear to ear.

I'm a bird that left a golden cage,
I dumped what hearts or bothers,
I loaned my loneliness to others;
They crave this masochistic rage.

I Lecture to Myself

During those sleepless nights
Under the wobbly candle lights,
I've read the books unknown,
Veiled on my life's bookshelf,
Today, I am quite grown,
I even lecture to myself:

"Be calm and sharp, aim well,
There is no second chance,
Don't fail to try to ring the bell,
Our life is a clever blender:
It effortlessly will handle
Such an old-fashioned dance.

Finish the journey of your life,
Send love to your best friends,
To every foe, to your ex-wife,
Shake a few neighbors' hands,
Then simply vanish, disappear,
Just leave your guilt and fear."

A shadow doesn't cast a tree,
Reality arranged it in reverse;
I lived in Hell before this glee,
I hate to trounce my own verse,
For heaven's sake,
Why don't I let it be?
Why can't I have
And eat the cake?

I Lost My Last Illusion

I was beguiled
By a conniving priest
Into one of the organized
Religions;
I didn't rise as dough
On a fresh yeast,
And walked away from
Brainwashed pigeons.

I lost my last illusion
And paid a heavy price,
My soul will never rise
Into a celestial fusion.

The wise forever learn,
The fools forever teach,
The sinners live in bliss
And flourish like a fern,
We dwell in the abyss
And torturously burn.

I leaned before my skis,
Unlocked our county jail,
Threw out rusty keys,
And lived to tell this tale.
There were two swans,
Authorities in hit-and-sack,
Amid the thieves and cons,
One white, the other black.

A white self-righteous swan
Coerced poor Leda to a kiss
And fell into a sizzling abyss.
A tainted, devilish black swan
Still preaches morality in bliss.

C'est la Vie

Some soar,
Some dive.
That's life.
Some fight and win,
Some lose a strife.
That's life.
Some are divorced,
Some have a lovely wife.
That's life.
Some beat the drums,
Some blow a fife.
That's life.
Some never worked,
Some work from 8 to 5.
That's life.
Some like the pageants,
Some think it is too rife.
That's life.
Some run and hide,
Some grab a falling knife.
That's life.
Some crossed the bridge
Of sorrows
Into the land of glee,
They'll rejoice tomorrows,
C'est la vie.

I Breathe

Glee inches into my dull existence
Under a gloomy overcast,
Only my conscience knows why
I don't deserve the glory wreath.
I am just revisiting my past,
Failing to run the bumpy distance,
But yet, I definitely breathe.

I met my first girlfriend last night,
"How have you been?
Is everything alright?"
"I'm doing reasonably well,
Along the blinding days and nights,
From misery into a garden of delights,
Sidestepping godsent bliss and Hell."

"I see no diamonds on tiny fingers,
I see no sapphires in your ears,
And yet, your godly beauty lingers,
In spite of quickly passing years."

"Thank you, take care, goodbye".
"Be good, stay cool; Bye-bye."

Only my conscience knows why,
I don't deserve the glory wreath;
She didn't say, "Don't be too shy,
I wish to see you soon, stop by",
And yet, I didn't die,
I breathe.

I Built a Cabin in the Woods

I built a cabin in the woods;
Please, enter with your smiles.
Come with your somber moods,
Get peace and quiet in your lives.

Enjoy my hearth with cozy flames,
Eat, drink and dance, be merry,
Love Mother Nature's games,
Enjoy its fruits and every berry.

It is a quick etude,
A modest revelation.
It is a nurtured solitude,
My gentle, quiet isolation;
I changed my feisty attitude,
I am still working on salvation.

A Bud Unfurls in just a Day

Our faces cast oblique expressions
Of a drained and burdened kindness,
Reflected in a dusty mirror on the wall
And in a teapot puffing on the stove.
My friends and I are casually drunk
Or rather cheerfully tipsy; loudly sharing
The latest funny jokes, unceremoniously
Interrupting and overpowering each other.
As always, we gathered in the kitchen,
My living room is loaded with antiques,
Too fragile for my well-oiled partners.

A bud unfurls in just a day,
A leaf turns yellow in one night,
Life flies by in a flash.
And yet, the flowers still sway,
The trees shed gold to our delight,
No one anticipates the dire crash.

If life is a perpetual theatre,
I'm definitely not an actor,
But an intelligent spectator.
A timid vaudeville just whistled by,
It is a lovely time to wave goodbye.

A Crystal Shrine

I listened to your farewell song
Plunging into me out of nowhere,
The words were deathly wrong,
Your heart was never there.

I liked the language of your book,
As sharp as your sarcastic mind,
I used a machete in every nook,
For the lies were tightly intertwined.

The ice masks our tiny creek
As if that wintry crystal shrine
Protects our family's mystique
From the Lord's piercing shine.

Your thoughts in every phrase
Remind me of a freezing lace
Or rather, of the dried bouquets
Forgotten in our marriage maze.

I hate small talk,
You toss the dice;
We couldn't walk
Into that river twice.

War's over: take your spoils,
Let's go our separate ways.
A watched pot never boils,
We've had much faster days.

A Sketch

A bundle of joy,
Its nature's ploy,
Gold of the leaves
Has piercing smells
Of a perfect ripeness,
The comfy water wells
Of our eternal kindness
Caress a window's frost,
Give liberty and restraint,
Knits lace for a holy ghost,
While winds of winter faint,
Until the melting snow leaks
Into the whisper of the creeks,
Across the fields dew-pearled,
To hail the seasons of the world.

I Asked my Death to Dance

A tiny drop of freedom
Worthy of a stream of years,
A path to a promised Eden
Paved with my bloody tears.

The victory came through
Flanked by two shiny rays,
I fought; I bled, but knew
I'll see the freedom grace.

The dusty broken mirrors
Buried the gloomy beams,
Only the brave, the heroes
Gave birth to sunny dreams.

The preachers of the word
Cook up or tickle our ears,
Warmongers of this world
Sow war and harvest fears.

The witch-hunt never stopped,
The brooms morphed into jets,
The shapeless future looms,
The bombs and rockets popped
And gentle brides and grooms
Grew into killed or injured vets.

It's not a jumpy decadence,
I like the turbulence in flight,
I asked my death to dance,
I like to tango before a fight.

I'm walking rickety tightrope,
I wasn't asked to like this life,
Hence, I'm in a bloody strife,

And marching utterly alone
Across this ravaged slope;
I'm a forbidden fruit in sight,
God, let them throw a stone,
It's better than the apple bite.

I Closed My Eyes

I'm like a weary deer,
Nailed by the swords
Of bright headlights.
I'm praying with no fear
And downhearted words
For peace without fights.

Dawn of the end of life,
Dusk of a futile strife;
I'm a philosopher tonight:
Life was a solitary dance;
My tunnel ends- there is no light;
Do I deserve another chance?
Do I deserve a second cherry bite?

Life wants to see me beg and crawl,
Death wants to see my final downfall.

I closed my eyes
To see the skies
Above the shores;
Only the dead
Have seen the end
Of bloody wars.

I Locked the Door into My Heart

I locked the door into my heart,
But you still keep the key.
If you can't bear being apart,
Just come and set me free.

A bouquet of roses in the snow,
The blood of my love-thirsty heart,
Sunset is rocking in the river's flow,
A cardinal is wounded by your dart.

Our love is like a leaky boat-
It sinks yet still remains afloat,
Even while in the quiet waters,
We sail together to the slaughters.

The truth is pure like our birth suit,
There is no need to stretch or bend;
The tree is known by its fruit,
Why are we fighting to the end?

Love is the ship of fools
Where everyone is blind,
For us, for two buffoons,
"Stop" is a useless sign.

I dwell no more on my lost fortune,
It was a nightmare boxed in torture,
I see an exit from my gloomy cage,
Life is a book-I simply turn the page.

A Blissful Ploy

My days devour shades of gray,
My nights get every sunny ray,
The evil drives the wedges
Between reality and our pledges.
The good just trims the hedge
To show off its shiny badge;
The losers had our late dinner,
A critic failed to pick a winner.

A girl stood on a bridge-
She didn't whine or cry,
She gave a defiant stare
And jumped to die.
I caught her in the air,
I heard her thankful sigh,
I saw her grace and flair.

We didn't want to kiss goodbye
Walking on that burning bridge;
A mirror of the wet asphalt
Echoed the scorching sky.
Our lives were under siege,
Our love crushed the assault.

It was a blissful ploy
Of my deflowered life,
I knelt. My endless joy
Agreed to be my wife.

A Farewell Swig

My nights still swim,
My days still drown,
My scotch is at the rim,
Begs to be taken down.
Where are you going?
I've been there.
You're just elbowing
My old nightmare.

You'll see my brothers, vets,
Deer-in-the-headlights looks,
Trudging along a shady path.
Their destinies placed bets
Not on some soldierly books,
But on the brutality of wrath.

Their souls' melodic keyboards
Seem feverishly eager
To play the horrifying chords
Of anthems for a trigger.

You'll see
A fascinating sight,
A world without lies,
You'll see
A sliver of moonlight
Part death and life.

My band is ready for a gig,
For a sad sound of the taps
Above their final port of call,
I'm ready for a farewell swig,
For Pyrrhic victories, no laps.

Maybe a requiem;
That's all.

A Departing Train

After the burning sun,
After its blinding glow,
I didn't choose to run,
I didn't choose to go.

Love turned
Into a lackluster flow,
An uninspiring trait
Of a departing train
Under a slothful rainbow
That bent too late,
After a penetrating rain.

Before the early snow,
Love kindly set me free
Into the woods of glee.
The trees already shed
Their multicolored gowns;
I brashly marched ahead
Onto the hollowed grounds.

But then I saw a latch
That slid into a groove
And locked the gates
Of paradise for sinners;
Thus no one evermore
Meets devils-saints
And losers-winners.

A Bad Dream

I whispered,
"I'm not like other men,
Say where and when,
Trust me, I'll be there,
All fair and square,
I'll never fail.
You're like my Holy Grail,
A little old, a little molded.
You judge and see ahead
You're not ever blinded,
You're just blindfolded.
You're my blinding light,
My singing nightingale,
You're my daily bread.
Oh, never mind,
I'll even learn the Braille
To have you for a night."

She said,
"Your love is not enough
To enter an erotic paradise,
I need a little more than love,
Just pay the asking price!"

I said,
"You're asking way too much,
A simple robbery won't help,
I let the others eat my lunch,
I'll live in misery and yelp,
I'll walk my shaded path,
Farewell, I'll hide my wrath."

My mind slept silently
Digesting awful news,
My always starving body
Escorted yet another muse.

Estranged

Winds ripped the smokes to shreds,
Sunflowers bent their yellow heads,
You wore a lacy wedding gown,
Like a swan dressed in silky down.

The angel of my life,
The sweetest honey of my hive,
So many moons have since passed by,
And still they're mourning our goodbye.

We flowed apart- estranged,
You wanted to be free,
But nothing really changed,
Even your photos didn't flee.

I was the willing victim of your love;
You seized my smiles and kisses.
You took my heart and flew away.
I wished you'd take me far above
Somewhere into the Milky Way,
Among a glee of hits and misses,
I was a willing victim of your love,
You seized my smiles and kisses,
You took my heart and flew away,
I wished you'd take me far above.

I had no happiness to lose,
Yet sadness filled my days,
You hung me in a noose-
Was it your last embrace?

Hemmingway

If one is cold-bloodedly gallant
And dwells in a graveyard shift,
It is quite easy to kill a talent;
It is so easy to bury a great gift.

Laconic, telegraphic lines;
A poetry of a magnetic prose;
He lived along his lines;
That's what he chose.

He drank that slick cocktail
Of lies and virtues,
He couldn't hide or veil
His constant tortures.

Man's poise is cheap,
Man's glee is more expensive,
At noon, he goes only for a sip,
At night, he becomes offensive.

The tales and cute fig leaves
No longer cover every night;
His words don't pass the sieves,
Life's tunnel doesn't have a light.

His world consumed with flames,
Don't waste on him your blames.

He loved a bitter-honey taste
Of drinks in his congested bar;
Forgive. His life was not a waste,
He was the greatest falling star.

Death pierced the branches
Then tossed away our fates;
His soul lives in the trenches,
His shotgun locked the gates.

I Love My Neighbor

A goddess or a god
Of a hard street labor,
Gave me a tender nod,
"You love your neighbor."

Beyond the fountains of glee,
Under the quilt of melancholy,
Years gladly drank her
As always bottoms up;
After the sticky liqueur
They passed that cup.

Whatever they have left,
Is good enough for me,
Her past wasn't a theft
Of lions from a menagerie.

The ship of fools moves fast
To push us through a sieve;
The ghosts of our shady past
Drain our thoughts and leave.

We patched the ugly holes
With anguish and disdain,
Then rinsed our tired souls
Under a passing rain.

Today, we both are bent
Below the weight of tears,
We had enough, but spent
Our riches draped in years.

A Cruel Hurricane

A cruel hurricane derails
Desires raked for today,
Only seagulls and sails
Enjoy the breeze's play.

Delusions fall apart,
I'll never live in glee,
You locked my heart
And threw away the key.

I love my solitude,
As life is a fine etude,
We're all the same
Under our skin,
No race, no fame,
Just kith and kin,
No guilt, no sorrows
Until the verdicts
Of tomorrows.

No accidental accidents
Set by a hungry science
Allow me to rest in peace
Draped by the immensity
Of silence,
And lulled by naked trees.

Along the River of Despair

I have no friends
They've all passed,
I have no enemies
At last,
I have no words to rhyme,
Only the mountains to climb,

The weak and stubborn camels
Order the pace of our caravans,
But I still flip the TV channels,
I have my independent plans,
Away from an ancient fashion,
Away from the wilted thoughts,
Away from the old and ashen,
Away from the Gordian knots.

I strode through thick and thin,
I'm wholly free, I have no skin
In the wars of our twisted idols.
The clowns of our sad days,
That pave a road to nowhere
Along the river of despair.

I'm a hawk, I circle in the sky,
But can no longer cherry-pick
The friends and enemies I like.
I keep my powder entirely dry,
I still don't need a walking stick,
Life is as dull as a hunger strike.

I have no friends,
They've all passed,
I have no enemies
At last.

A Bird of Hope

I am numb-
I am a paper dove-
I am a bird of hope-
I am a bird of love-
I am dumb-
I am a bird of dope.

A lifeless sunlight moaned
Until a miraculous nightfall.
Ever so often, I am stoned,
Life is a rapture free-for-all.

I had a dreadful thought,
A masochist's delight;
It wasn't a victory I sought,
I craved to lose the fight.

I lost some victories,
I won a few defeats,
I turned those mysteries
Into the sweetest treats.

Sometimes, I spread my wings
And hover just above the trees,
Alone, without queens or kings,
Toward the happy end of rope
To watch the truth's striptease.

I am an angel of undying hope.

Enlightened Failure

A bunch of psychedelic strangers
Holds signs: "Make Love, Not War".
They long and march for peace,
They fight, but only war arranges
Their fallen shadows on the floor
As if it is their destiny's caprice.

Numb silence shuts the door.
A spoken word is just a lie;
They make both love and war
And hear their mothers' cry.

Affairs erased their fear,
Love wore a velvet glove.
They dreamed of being here;
They wanted to be slaves of love.

They tried to balance loss and gain,
Their intentions overlapped.
They ran towards the end of pain;
Their wounds were never wrapped.

Stars fell on their hot heads,
Smiles cheered their faces,
They lived like jolly newlyweds,
Caged in their own embraces.

Enlightened failure of eternal glory
Depends on where I end this story.
Delusions of the future are in hands
Of those who paid the marching bands

Don't Rush to Bury Me

I am a victim of suspicion,
My flesh is scarred,
My soul is masked;
It is my egotistic mission,
I am a lackluster bard
Until I am in grandeur basked.

I cast no shadow on the ground,
Even the vultures stare at me,
But I am for glory clearly bound,
Don't rush to bury me.

Don't count my net worth,
Don't move into my room,
It is your fantasy and froth,
I'm in glee; you're in gloom.

If you'll notice I am dead,
Start your devouring flame,
Try to be jolly; not so sad,
Burn me, I'll take the blame.

Just lock that gate,
Toss what I earned
Into the lake of love
Or in the sea of hate,
I am already burned,
I've seen enough…

Eludes those Cracking Whips

A grossly plumaged horse
Eludes those cracking whips
Under the tent of our circus.
If someone buys and pours,
Somebody always sips
Then runs in hellish circles.

As this ill-treated horse,
I try to reach the borders
Of liberation every night.
I write my caustic verses,
Even the Holy orders
Remain eternally finite.

In vain, I try to comb our lives,
I try to recreate a ruthless play
Of falling stars and knives
That leave the Milky way.

My stanzas' crooked mirrors
Fail to unchain themselves;
Their nervous bookish heroes
Die on the dusty shelves.

Those heroes' marble tombs
Stand like the barren wombs,
So sad and fruitlessly nocturnal,
Knowing that nothing is eternal.

Eternal Adolescence

True love strikes our hearts,
And lovers chirp like sparrows
Among Illusions at first sight;
And cupids send their darts,
While Venus sends her arrows
And no one stops their flight.

I fill two glasses to the rims.
I kiss your gorgeous face.
You are an icon of my whims,
I gleam in your embrace.

Today, the thrill is gone,
Today, love stops its flow,
Today, I'm the only one
Who doesn't know.

Two wounded hearts
That used to beat as one
Can't fix the broken parts
That harmony has gone.

Two thoughtless seagulls fly
Above the nervous sea,
Empathy tries to pass us by
Alongside our wilted glee.

Love was a horseless carriage,
It brought our vanity and pride
Among the pains of marriage,
Along the shaky tiresome ride.

Love faded as an ancient myth,
Within our eternal adolescence,
Only a plastic wedding wreath
Learned from the bitter lessons.

Don't Try to Fly

Eyes, ears and brains,
Each just a useless organ,
Nobody undertones a word
On life's abandoned trains.
The passengers are gone,
They left their timid world
To listen to a lethal silence
With their exhausted feet
Across the chill and heat
Without moral guidance.

I am alone against the wall,
Farewell, red-hot Beirut,
You burn my weary soul,
I keep my wartime loot:
A decorated wooden duck,
A portrait of a prostitute,
A stuffed ten-pointer buck,
A good-luck Ginseng root.

If you're born to crawl,
Don't tease yourself,
Don't ever try to fly.
It's not your downfall;
Just climb on your bookshelf,
Let greatness pass you by.

Lives fly and whistle in the air
Like prehistoric arrowheads,
Between illusions and despair,
The Gods still pull the threads.

A Day Before

My angel blew the golden horn;
He wants another bloody war.
Boys will be born;
They fight, then die and soar.

Please, tell my Mom and Dad,
It's war. I'll knock on wood.
Don't cry; don't bother,
I'll return alive or dead.
Life is a brotherhood
Of war and sex,
One substitutes the other,
Boys drown in this life's vortex.

I trail my angel by a few feet,
Six feet below the ground,
Both knowing we will meet
When I'm gone hell bound.

A day before,
I'll see you, a winged friend,
I'll kick your ass and chin,
Then start a daily trend.
I'll curse you for the war,
Then readjust your ugly grin.

I have returned
With a backpack of worries.
My soldier's fate u-turned,
If that's not a reward, what is?

Back to the bar,
A little better is a foe of good,
I hope I can afford this whim.
A single barrel, if you would,
A hefty snifter to the rim,
Bartender, you're damn good.

As Punishment for Debts

God gave, God took;
No one could say it better.
I freeze like an English setter
And feel the morning breeze
Before I read the Holy Book
To know forest from the trees.

Forgiveness comes
As punishment for our debts,
Ostensible as pompous gifts
Or gaming houses' high bets
Failing to fill my bad luck rifts.

I'm fence-mending;
It's tough: I'm in pain.
My isolation never-ending,
I can no longer feel
The pain of others,
As if I'm in the slow lane.
One hand is on the wheel,
The other flips the birds,
Avoiding extra dirty words
About our beloved mothers.

Curved mirrors of my soul,
My biased mind and eyes
Don't see beyond the hole
In front of earthly paradise.

I always spot
The wolves and their foul habits,
Their horrid quests and tasks.
I hardly spot
The cute, saint-hearted rabbits
Behind their uninspiring masks.

No one can see a ragtag crowd
And spot the one who left for us
His shroud.

A Drifter

I hummed "Amazing Grace",
Somebody killed my heart;
I miss a well forgotten art,
The warmth of an embrace.

I slog across each state
From Florida to Maine,
Devoted to a drifter's fate,
Whether it is shine or rain.

I roam with unimportant guys,
Trading some dated dirty jokes;
I eat my burgers 'n french-fries,
We're happy clams. No yokes.

My exodus was not a liberation;
I claim no places as my own.
My train already left the station,
I will explore my curiosity alone.

Today, I'm hiking to the West
From San Diego to Seattle,
Enjoying weed and all the rest
While looking for a lighter battle.

I heard some other drums;
I trudged to distant beats;
I marched across the slums,
The only victory in my defeats.

My past became a total blur,
My future did not show up,
The heavens heard my slur,
"Goddamn it, pass that cup."

A Cube of Sugar

A vicious rain passed by,
I heard its angry whisper,
"Don't ever cross my path;
Did you enjoy your bath?"
A rainbow said bye-bye,
Its voice was drier, crisper.

I want a little sugar
In my glee,
Don't be too frugal.
I want a little darkness
In my tea,
Don't be too heartless.
For you
The color of despair
Is grayish blue,
But I've been there
And it was black.
Tonight, I start anew,
I'm back.
Trust me, don't doubt,
I gamble; I often tout.

An early evening in a casino,
File mignon, a glass of Pinot,
Then comes on my checklist,
Espresso with a lemon twist,
A cube of sugar on the side,
The night is young; let's ride.

I saw another rain,
I crossed its path;
You said it was in vain,
But I enjoyed its wrath.

From Truth to Lies

We see small splinters
In everybody's eyes,
We miss big logs in ours.
We live and take U-turns
From truth to lies
During the darkest hours.

At times, we look alive,
And even act like winners,
Some say, we just survive
To lay to rest our dinners.

Dissecting every hair
Obscures our minds.
Amid our stars and crosses,
Reality is hard to bear.
We find our losses,
But lose our finds.

Uncertainty is on the rise,
Cold winters never ask,
Winters break-in.
Integrity is a surprise
While we still bask
In a passed autumn's grin.

Another winter
Consumed us for a song,
Next year, we'll be ready,
Am I too wrong?

History isn't a Teacher

History isn't a teacher,
But a cruel prosecutor
That punishes all those,
Who didn't learn its lessons.

I'm drinking from a firehose
The choppy waters of my confusions,
I can no longer understand the youth;
Maybe the history just puts my nose
Into the world of optical illusions,
And I assume that I may see the truth.

Forget the nuts and bolts,
The brick and mortar,
The tooth and nail...
I'm sure, the future holds
And wants to flip that quarter
Which will allow me to win or fail.

What is the end-all of my life?
Is it the dead-end of my road?
Is it a U-turn on my street?
Is it a quiet cul-de-sac
Of an eternal coexistence
With those who bored me
All my lifelong daily strive?

The never-ending yesterdays
Keep me between the exodus
And a concluding destination.
I'm a tiny star that left the sky
For the infinity of a frustration.

History is a smart bookkeeper;
Our experience is just a yoke.
I'll fly higher and dig deeper,
I'll never crawl, I'll go for broke.

An Empty Terminal of Love

Fates are unjust,
Some live to see sunset;
Some die before sunrise,
Some love, some only lust,
Some dwell in paradise,
Some fall into a spider's net.

My name is on the list;
My lady calls it black,
I'm a hell-bound beast,
I run my noosing track.

She shows herself in,
As I show myself out;
She sports adrenalin,
I'm too vain and proud.

I'm an empty terminal of love;
I'm a train that left the station,
She thinks it's just my bluff,
And puts me on probation.

It's just an odd affair,
I love her, nonetheless.
I simply can no longer bear
Her everlasting monologue.
She thinks she is a princess,
She thinks I am a frog.

And Wilted Red Roses' Petals

I'm tired of being scared,
I'm scared of being tired,
I'd like to have the power
Of some tyrannical kingmakers.
Even my doubles of a happy hour
Don't lead me through God's acres,
Where our ideas are never shared,
Where self-esteem isn't required.

My sudden swirls of daily struggles
Confuse my foes but cast the pearls
Before the pencil-pushing muggers
And keep their future on its toes.

My living is a job worth doing right.
Cord-cutting the arrogance of youth
Will stop decay and shed the light
On what we speak of as the truth.

Life's marching to the end,
And I'm pulling back my horns
Into a box with my old medals.
I buried my last friend:
He rests under the feisty thorns
And wilted red roses' petals.

Most can't appreciate filigree
In precious fragments of my soul;
Most only see the cruelty of sins,
Among the finest lace of old intrigues,
While dim nuances drown in the whole,
And life's disdain erases my small role,
In the prevailing views of the society
As a critique on intellectual anxiety.

Eternal Tango

She is a nightclub striptease dancer,
Undressed like forests in the winter.
I am a ruthless tattooed bouncer,
A sentimental brute, a loner-drifter.

Let's put ourselves to work,
Put on your dancing shoes;
I'll lead you to the road's fork.
What's next? You choose.

Just follow my right palm;
Make your enticing moves.
Use your disarming charm
Along the tango grooves.

We'll dance our way
Between the tables
Into a happy day
From our grim fables.

Two souls, one pain;
Two loves, one ploy;
Two lines, one lane
Into our endless joy.

The tango of two doves,
The harbor of two loves,
The tango of two lives
Into eternal paradise.

At Times

The birds are singing,
The trees are growing.
Old friends turn on a dime
Or fight with my upbringing.
I write my verse unknowing
That mediocrity and talent
Never rhyme.

My rather convoluted DNA
Can't coexist with that of others.
At times, we are above the fray,
At times, we blame our mothers.

At times my rambling mind,
Repeats slipups already fined,
At times, I auction out our lies,
I'm a holler; I'm a coronel,
But my muse only rolls her eyes,
And my dismay remains eternal.

At times a flame devours me
That burns my daily bread.
Today, our life won't be the same,
I'm a needle: you're the thread.

Don't look for pluses
And minuses in me,
I'm not your Duracell.
Don't eat my lunch,
Don't petal my canoe
Don't grade my paper.
I wish you well,
I'll see you later.

Farewell, Dear Sun

This prison is my cradle-
I never see another world-
The sky is sliced in four-
The bars run to the gable,
A sharp Damoclean sword
Carves shadows on the floor.

It is a box of great Pandora,
I'm in the Forbidden City,
I hear the echo of Gomorrah,
I'm the one to sign a treaty.

I'm not un conducteur Dimanche,
I carve my verses every day,
Trust me, I earned carte blanche
For anything I write or say.

My verses drift
Across the sky,
It is my humble gift,
It is my last goodbye.

A common sense
Offended,
I'm ready for a better world,
I cocked my gun,
My usefulness
Has ended,
Just take my somber word,
Farewell, dear Sun.

Graffiti

Please, take a shower.
It's not a time for glory;
Don't throw in the towel,
I'm here to tell the story.

The rite of spring,
My lazy morning stroll,
The birds don't sing,
I read graffiti on the wall,
"Unjustly written law
Isn't my law,
At all.
Not every problem
Is a nail,
Not every solution
Is a hammer,
We fail to trust,
We choose to bail,
A jail is not a must,
Unlock the slammer."

The jailed birds don't sing
Even for the rite of spring.

Don't Torture Me

You weep; I feel your pain.
You lose, I cannot gain.
I hope your dignity still flies
Above your cunning cries.

I can no longer see your hollow eyes ;
Just set me free, devour your own lies.
Don't torture me, leave me alone,
I sail the tidy sea; I am tired, I am worn.

Don't torture me, the star must shine
Above the Christmas tree and I am fine.

Don't torture me, don't hide your moves,
March vis-à-vis, along these grooves.

Don't torture me, I tried my very best,
I found my own glee; I reached the crest.

Don't torture me, don't clip my wings,
Like Icarus, I flee to Saturn's rings.

Don't torture me, don't shake the salt,
While beer is free, I drink my single malt.

Don't torture me, get out; lock the door,
Throw away the key; Enough. No more.

Don't torture me,
No one above my head,
I'm not a saint; You've been misled.

Good Wars

A bullet flew, I couldn't duck it;
Survived to sail the sea of glee
For more than eighty years.
Those flashes kicked the bucket.
But I'm annoyed; I'm not a devotee
Of those who only shed their tears.

So-called good wars are worse
Than any fragile truce or peace.
Warmongers fight without reasons.
I wish we put them on their knees,
Then lock them up in prisons,
Until their heartless cruelly will cease.

I heard from one pathetic preacher,
"War's pretty tough, yet it's a teacher."
Response was accurate, but coarse,
"You only preach! We bleed in wars!"

Downfall

My poetry is on the ropes,
Unkindly plagued with guilt,
I try to tailor startling hopes
And fresh ideas for its quilt.

Right at the crack of noon,
Pursuing nonexistent crimes,
I am creating my own moon,
Gleaming above my rhymes.

My lines echo a dated fashion,
Wolfed by the hungry flames
Of my unanswered passion
Confronting critics' blames.

I am suffocating in a world
Of anti-intellectual quagmire.
That's why I hone my sword
While preaching to the choir.

Short years of wisdom gaze
Over my long-misguided life,
That marches at a slow pace,
Unstoppable as a falling knife,
Fearing its sparkling downfall
In premonition of a final brawl.

Ascended Spirit

An ascended spirit
Lands on our Earth;
I vigorously veer it
Into another berth,
Into another youth,
Into life's only truth.

Now, I am resurrected.
It is a gift I had to earn,
My role is not affected,
Just wait, I shall return.

Meanwhile, I am in bliss,
A state of the unknown,
I took a penname Chris
And carved it on a stone.

Then told the fallen angel,
"Our rivalry can't thrive
From light to darkness,
Let's cease this awful strife,
And never fight in vain.
I realize your odds remain
The darkest."

Lives end with death;
We hear the requiems
Of Mozart, Verdi, Brahms,
But hold your breath,
I save the sacred flames
Of Mathew's psalms.

Lively Equilibrium

The lively equilibrium of Calder's mobile
Conveys a rather fragile peace of mind,
Like peace between the poor and noble,
Though they are stanchly intertwined.

I'm pushed by moneyed art collectors,
Those who have so-called holistic views,
But I prefer to march among the debtors
As long as they are not insipid hues.

Please, stay away from me,
It is entirely my fault,
Don't use your cookie-cutter;
The sausages got made.
Please, let me be.
I missed the treasure vault,
I stayed in my relaxing gutter,
Somebody else got paid.

Predictability
Props instability and death,
The end of innocence,
The parting baby's breath.
The start of human liability
For our lackluster, dreadful lives
That veer amid the falling knives.

Only dense, well-mended fences
Make decent neighbors,
Even the rattling drums and sabers,
Even the rags-to-riches dreams
Don't wake me in the morning.
But I still take my humble chances;
My life prefers caressing beams,
Just comfortably warm, not burning.

Don't Spin the Globe

Don't spin the globe,
Don't waste my time,
I'm a claustrophobe
Chained to my rhyme.

The futile human rules
Own millions of acres
Of Heaven for the mules,
And Hell for lawmakers.

We're down to the wire;
We argue day and night,
About smoke without fire,
About wrong and right.

Life flaunts in front of me
A never-ending futile strife;
I am a man, who never flee,
I am a bee that lost his hive.

Life broke a sacred ban
Of Eve's forbidden bite.
I am like a wicked man,
I'd rather love than fight.

Don't Lose Your Head

Cherchez la femme.
You learn
Intentions of the Lamb;
You earn
Perceptions of the day.
Beware:
Don't travel far away;
She's waiting in your bed.
Quite rare:
Don't lose your head.

Remember Salome in dance,
John's head bled on a plate,
She wouldn't take a glance,
She knew the Baptist's fate.

Here's a tiny hair I'd like to split,
Perhaps for someone's benefit:
Don't cast the first and only stone;
Wait for the others to participate
And keep in mind the gaudy fable.
One day, you could be left alone,
Performing on the table
Or bleeding on the plate.

Don't Try to Fly

Eyes, ears and brains,
Each just a useless organ,
Nobody undertones a word
On life's abandoned trains.
The passengers are gone,
They left their timid world
To listen to a lethal silence
With their exhausted feet
Across the chill and heat
Without moral guidance.

I am alone against the wall,
Farewell, red-hot Beirut,
You burn my weary soul,
I keep my wartime loot:
A decorated wooden duck,
A portrait of a prostitute,
A stuffed ten-pointer buck,
A good-luck Ginseng root.

If you're born to crawl,
Don't tease yourself,
Don't ever try to fly.
It's not your downfall;
Just climb on your bookshelf,
Let greatness pass you by.

Lives fly and whistle in the air
Like prehistoric arrowheads,
Between illusions and despair,
The Gods still pull the threads.

The Infantile Desire

A self-assured stupidity
Beats our intellects and doubts,
It has been known from infinity,
A gentle silence dies in shouts.

We entertain the infantile desire
To reinvent the past,
To use a garden hose
And wash the ugly and the dire
Or try to recompose
The parables that couldn't last.

A comedy of childish nihilism
Merged with unmasked fascism,
The curtains fall and theatres
Vanish,
Even the innocence of actors
Is venomously punished.

I wonder if I'm still an actor;
I wonder if there's a role to learn.
I wonder if our love is still a factor;
I wonder if our hearts still burn.

Our love was flanked
With crooked mirrors,
And thus we parted,
No one was blamed or thanked,
Even the passing rivers
Didn't caress the brokenhearted.

Blind self-assured stupidity
Blocked our path into infinity.

As a Pinch of Salt

We wear a scarlet letter,
A punishment of a desire,
Sunset is always better
Than a ball of fire.

We never miss the city beat,
We're guiltier than seven sins.
Two hills will never meet,
There is a gap no one can fill;
Too many losses and no wins,
The cause of our morbid thrill.

We are like a zigzagged bolt
Of a blinding lightning.
The thunders are exciting,
And yet there is a better day,
Just as a pinch of salt.
It is much harder to burn out,
And slowly fade away,
Than never have a doubt.

External inconsistencies
Don't stop us at the doors.
We cross unfriendly seas
And start our bloody wars.

Nobody dwells in Eden.
Forget the soapy fairytales;
Our evils are well-hidden,
They jumped their bails.

We see the darkest hour
Of silence before dawn.
Life is a wilted flower,
It dies and we are gone.

Don't Strew Your Salt

Don't strew your salt
Over my aching wound,
It is not somebody's fault,
That lives are not attuned.

Our hearts are cold,
We drink away our love,
The rest is put on hold,
Enough is not enough.

We climb the hills
To see the daily light,
Then sign our sulky wills
And leave without a fight.

Even the go-getting bulls
Crawl into a golden cave,
It is inertia without rules,
An invitation to the grave.

The waterfalls of rains
Run into the sea of live,
They channel our veins
Into another futile strive.

It is a time of dancing bears,
Of carnivals and fire-eaters,
Of acrobats on their trapezes,
Of gorgeous, naughty girls
To race in their two-seaters
Against the morning breezes.

Our snugly anchored hearts
Each wears a gloomy mask,
Our dullness hides the mirth,
Our reality imitates the arts,
Sad, morbid and grotesque,
Yet, hung above this Earth.

War Is Hell

Humiliated and unmasked,
At the beginning of the end,
To save my life, I am asked
By Evil to betray my friend.

Life's like a train,
I ride alone without a friend,
My ticket wins a life's dead end.
In vain,
I pray under the weight of life,
Like Isaac
Under his Father's knife.

Today, I am on my own,
My life is in my hands,
I brashly blow my horn
In the marching bands.

The winters chill my soul,
They freeze my weary heart,
And yet I reach my only goal,
I treat my life as a work of art.

When I hear Thy Father
Or when I meet His Son,
My fallen friends will gather,
They made that hole-in-one.

Farewell, my Gallant Matador

The squeaky trunks of trees
Sway slowly in a scorching wind,
The sun is hiding in the leaves
Like a teen-ager who has sinned.

The spiders weave their lace,
Long branches scratch the sky
Unruly twigs try to embrace,
It's hot, even the birds don't fly.

I'm in Barcelona, Spain.,
I watch the Catalonian night.
I watch the opulence of pain;
I watch the last bullfight.
I watch the matadors jaywalk;
I watch a bloody, shaken bull;
I listen to a heartless squawk,
I hold a drink; my glass is full.

Dusk pulls the sun away,
No one can save the day.
The sky is burning,
The southern night
Without a warning,
Turns off the light.

Farewell, my gallant matador,
A merciless mockery no more.
Farewell to that majestic bull,
Which kept my wineglass full.

I Am a Verses-Weaver

The men in dark and filthy robes
Judge our deeds and prosecute,
We don't accept their twisted probes,
We scream, only the dead are mute.

Boys died, the truth was fudged
Their wives and mothers cried,
But those who sent them there
Were never disciplined or judged.

We knew some of the dead firsthand,
The fallen were the same, but paler,
We tried to occupy somebody's land.
A lifelong common avenue of failure.

Today, my life is just a sleepy river,
What happens when the river dries?
I won't survive; I am a verses-weaver,
I'll die. No one will ever read my lies.

Today, I wear my own big shoes,
I have my own low hanging habits,
I drink my single barrel booze,
I lose and laugh while others grieve,
I showoff my hat with a few rabbits,
But pull four aces from my sleeve.

For better or for worse,
I am living in my verse.
We'll be judged. God later saves,
We'll be equal only in the graves.

Don't Open Yet The Gate

Silver runs through my hair,
As if the snow coats the trees,
I'm not ready for my last affair,
I hope my pain is just a tease.

Under the grandeur of the sky,
Above the riches of this land;
It's not my time to die,
I trust it's not the end.

My cellar is quite full,
My friends are all alive;
The markets run a bull,
I can still drink and drive.

So many songs I haven't heard,
So many books I haven't read,
I want to sing like a mockingbird,
I crave a gorgeous girl in bed.

No one yet knows when to hold,
No one yet knows when to fold,
Don't open yet the gate,
Don't even wait, for I'll be late.

Far Back, As I Can Remember

Far back, as I can remember,
I dreamed about Heaven,
I knew the Ten Commandments,
Sometimes eleven.
Just mark my word,
The real faith is a terrific gift,
I asked to see a better world,
God heard. I hope he's got my drift.
I see His weightless presence in the air;
He floats and doesn't touch the ground.
My hair turns gray, I shiver and I swear,
But everything is lit and gleams around.
His wavy hair looked like a golden rye,
His sparkly eyes were like a melted sky,
My thoughts were pulled from the abyss,
At last, I have arrived to rest in peace.
His words rang like a thunder in my head,
I recognized the voice and His demeanor,
"Remember, Son ", He passionately said,
"Your neighbor's grass is always greener!"
He washed my sins away;
My soul is happy being His,
The angels show me the way
Into eternity of promised bliss.
The sun will never leave the sky,
The flowers are blooming all year round,
We quietly dwell here - my Lord and I,
But I'm completely boredom-bound.
I walk between the sunny rays;
I see the grandeur of the World,
I miss my human yesterdays
While living with my Lord.
I've had few hurdles on my track,

At last, I reached my Paradise,
But why do I think of going back
And hide from Him my teary eyes?
"My Lord", one day I humbly say,
"I'm too bored; I think I'll faint,
Sometimes I miss being sad,
I'm still a human, not a saint."
He looked at me with empathy and smiled,
Then touched my face and said, "My Son,
I'll let you go back to Earth. Be madly wild,
Enjoy yourself until the fun has gone."
I'm back on Earth and all of that,
The same old boozy cheers and smiles,
We eat, we drink; we chew the fat.
I want to go back. I miss my Paradise.

French Crepe

French crepe shines like the moon
On a cast-iron skillet of the night,
Coquettish stars invite my spoon
Into their paradise for every bite.

I like the nights when spongy clouds
Remind of St. Agur, a bleu fromage.
Calva of Normandy, without doubts,
To you I'm writing this homage.

I'm absolutely sentimental, yet sincere-
It's just a lunch, c'est a mourir de Plaisir.
Champagne, superior growth Pinot Noir,
It's even better than my lover's boudoir.
Coquilles, crevettes, tarte à l'oignon,
Cuisses de grenouilles, fraiche galette,
Pomme frites, jambon fait a la maison,
Flambee Chambord on crepes Suzette.

In Sparta, all of us who ate to live
Were pushed straight off the cliff.
Long live the epicures and sybarites:
All those who live for drinks and eats.

Another Requiem

This isn't a requiem
For souls without cages,
For thieves without prisons,
For poetry without pages,
Or churches without whores.
It's just a requiem
For lives without aspirations,
For sins unknown to remorse,
Saved by a statute of limitations.

Autumn strolls
Across the fields,
Forgiven memories of souls
Fly high above the yields,
On a quest for the inevitable end
Of this intoxicating flight,
Where foe becomes your friend
Tip-toeing to the light.

I dare to shut off all the daily lights,
With a bird sitting on my shoulder,
Watching pole dancers on TV.
I dive into the eternity of nights.
My name lives in St. Paul's folder,
And navigates the roads of glee.

It is a requiem
For a friendless passenger
Riding the train named Life.
It's for the disillusioned messenger
Escaping from a vicious strife.

It is a requiem for those
Who knew such ruthless force;
Who missed the golden fleece;
Who've dreamt of peace,
But saw the end of wars.

Almost Iambic Sonnet

Self-evident compulsions and deliriums
Of uninvited brutal nouveau riche artillery,
Unbalance the fragile olden equilibriums
Of sculptures in the Jardin des Tuileries.

I have a tiny place in France,
A graveyard of depressions,
A festive funeral for our griefs.
A faux poster of Toulouse-Lautrec
Reminds me of those wicked days
When I would gladly stick my neck
Out of ancient Parisian walkways
To take a longer, deeper glance
At trees attaining autumn fashions
Of elegantly falling golden leaves.

Above My Melancholic Eyes

I downed milk from every star,
The Milky Way declared a war.
I'm back; I set my hair aflame
To warm my snifter in the bar.
The public left and shut the door,
Until I get a little bit more fame,
Until I pawn my wedding ring,
Until a voiceless swan will sing,
Until I drink myself to death,
Until they hear my final breath.

I asked "Our Father…",
And wasn't heard or just ignored,
I asked "Our Mother…",
But she already cut that cord.
Nobody answered from the skies,
The falling angel didn't try to stop
The requiem ascended to the top
Above my tired melancholic eyes.

I never fed the hungry;
I never clothed the naked;
I failed to flaunt my empathy.
I tried, but couldn't fake it.

I ran from Pyrrhic victories in life
Into the space where wisdom
Crossed the influence of times.
Where a well-reasoned word
Ruined the orbit of a falling knife,
Where our brittle principles
Aren't turning on the dimes,
Where science overrules the Lord,
Where no one locks the doors,
Where even the living
See the end of wars.

The Olden Drawbridge is Set Apart

The olden drawbridge is set apart,
Two heartlessly alienated silhouettes
Of loving swans were foully stopped
From following their daily etiquettes.

They wanted just a "neck and kiss",
While a tall ship is being navigated;
They loved their silent modest bliss,
Their peace was viciously invaded.

I hope their love affair goes on,
They aren't ready for their songs,
Those melodies are yet unborn,
Until they hear the angels' horns.

The olden drawbridge is set apart
Against the gentle lights of dawns,
A charming masterpiece of art,
Two chiseled silhouettes of swans.

Waterfalls of Vanity

I sing to earn my beer,
Smoke chokes the bar,
Nobody wants to hear
The cries of my guitar.

Hey, barman, tell me the truth
Straight as the strings of rain;
I suffered greatly in my youth,
Do I deserve a day without pain?

My castles in the sky won't fall;
They never heard about gravity.
They entertain my mind and soul
With tempting waterfalls of vanity.

Dire nightmares left my bed.
I can enjoy my morning ride,
Yet I'm hanging by a thread
Of interwoven vanity and pride.

I'll ignore the warning signs,
I'll navigate the twilight zone,
I'll dream between the lines,
But carve my poetry in stone.

A Bitter Teardrop

A tiny snowflake isn't a snowfall,
But yet a teardrop is a waterfall.

I run into my own tomorrow,
The gods must let me know,
To be or not to be;
To fade today or live in glee.
I run toward the urban noise
From fatal, chocking silence;
Nobody hears my voice
Nobody wants my guidance.

They fondly chew the fat,
This cunning hollow foam
Of our political correctness;
I have no rabbits in my hat.
I'm living in a nursing home,
Dismayed by my erectness.

I'm not waving plastic flags;
I've been around: I'm grown up.
It's quite impertinent of some
To stick these puny rags
Into my face, but I'm not a pup,
I buy and chew my own gum.

I'm sick of giving olive branches.
It hurts to turn the other cheek.
I would prefer to fight in trenches
Than play a childish hide n' seek.

I'm sick of being pushed around,
I give a hand; they grab my arm.
Yet I'm honesty and glory bound,
I'm a doctor sworn to do no harm.

149

A Blindfolded Goddess

A blindfolded lady
Can't see the light,
Can't see my face,
Although my name is in her hat,
I quietly descend the staircase,
Wrapped in a blanket of the night.
I'm hiding from my next combat,
For her, I'm not yet shovel-ready.

I used to be a one-man band
In a silence of bureaucracy;
I sailed across our fertile land
Along the tides of mediocrity.

Today, I'm at the edge of life.
I taught my dearest friends
To ring the church's bell.
I'm a forgotten rusted knife,
A burning candle from both ends,
Writing the words of my farewell.

Murmuring mourners
Slowly parading, dressed in black
As signs of imminent decay.
Life was a square without corners.
I paced my distance of that track,
It is a perfect time to call the day.

A blindfolded lady was a fraud,
And sped ahead into the past.
I stepped before a firing squad
Into sweet memories that last.

A Boring Carnival

I missed my parting shot,
And quickly left the stage,
A prima ballerina I am not,
I have no golden cage.

I can no longer catch the bus,
I hardly ever bark or bite.
Nevertheless, I lie and cuss,
Then blame the blinding light.

Life knows
Who's who and what's what.
We're fighting
For our places at the table.
We disregard the olden times
Of Cain and Able.
Neglecting poetry and prose.
We win the throne
Then lose the crown.
We shake the trees and watch,
But nothing's falling down.

The sun is falling downwards,
The shadows grow longer
Into a total darkness;
Life morphs into a paradise
Without flowers and birds;
Into a boring, endless carnival
Without brazen loud barkers.

Arbeit Macht Frei

We can't forgive. We hate
The words on hellish gate;
The labor frees. Obey.
"Arbeit macht frei"

Defenseless millions go in,
But few come out.
An unforgivable and heinous sin
Against the chosen and devout.

"Arbeit macht frei"
The shepherds guard their prey,
The walking shadows of the Jews.
Even the Gods have no excuse.

We heard their bitter sighs,
We felt their hopeless tears,
We saw a question in their eyes,
Unanswered through the years.

It's written by ancient scribes,
About diamonds in the rough,
About suffering, but pious tribes;
Eternal love for them is tough.

"I've chosen just a few,
Don't ever touch my hoard
Or I shall punish you,"
Pronounced the Lord.

Don't worry, please,
"Arbeit macht frei"
The labor frees.
God's Judgment day
Arrived too late
For that satanic gate.

An Etude

My path in life is clean and slick,
It veers just past the dirty ditches.
I'm an expert village chiropractor,
But if you fall and slash your dick,
I'm not trained to do the stitches,
You'll have to call a real city doctor.

Jesus pulled this old man back to life,
Poor Lazarus enjoyed his resurrection,
But was abandoned by his angry wife,
She said, "I lost the joy of his erection."

The evident morale of this etude
Is obvious, yet not too frequent,
If Jesus brings you back, my dude,
Demand a comprehensive treatment.

I Left Behind My Cheating Church

I went to church for Eucharist
To see a newly drafted priest,
His past was cleanly husked,
I prayed a little bit and asked:
"Why are you so kindly lenient
With those who always cheer?
Why can't you bring the quiet
To tell the truth without fear?"
His mass was vastly strewn
With countless sugared lies;
He shook and brashly threw
The forged and crooked dice.
Maybe for skeptics it's a fiction,
I scraped my gains and losses,
Hence on the day of crucifixion,
I found Christ amid the crosses.
The kisses sent, the ribbons torn,
A miracle has ripened to be born,
My soul has reached the Lord,
A bond nobody craves to scorch,
Delivered me into a better world.
I left behind my cheating church.

A Gift

I played as often as I could,
She loved me, loved me not.
At first, it was quite good
And then it was not.

An awful wrongness
Crawled into my head;
It was my loneliness,
It was my daily bread.

I couldn't bear the stress,
But wouldn't fight it whatsoever,
It's like a tacky wedding dress,
Uninteresting, but kept forever.

She never called me sir,
She kept me like a dog.
To my sincere dismay,
For her it was in vogue;
I always heard from her,
Heel, eat, sit, roll or stay.

My life was lived,
But slowly got much worse.
I gave myself a needed gift,
I filed for divorce.

A lost paradise was found,
Again, I am happy, all alone,
No friends, nor foes around,
I am a hound on the bone.

A Guided Ride

I saw the dawn in your alluring eyes
I soared into the morning skies,
To reach my soul that's been away
Since the Last Judgement Day.

I found, much to my dismay
That souls were heavily disheveled,
The crystal ball was artfully beveled,
And I couldn't find Heaven's stairway.

I'm sure, there will be choppy waters
Before my journeys end,
I'll live through wars and slaughters,
I'll watch our gods and heroes bend.

My life's a constant scrimmage
To calm my draining stress,
To keep my vanity in check.
I just promote my image
Of a couldn't-care-less
Tough-talking old redneck.

I'm back to my Parisian walkways,
A gray-haired tour to the D'Orsey,
A guided ride on a windy riverboat.
I love these magic nights and days,
This gorgeous all-you-can-eat buffet,
A venom that won't need an antidote.

A Burning Red-Hot Grille

Sunsets caress the sphinx,
The ruler of eternal sands.
He never sleeps or blinks,
While I scrutinize his lands.

Life's still a tragic vaudeville,
A parody of gods and sinners,
A burning red-hot grille
For guiltless young beginners.

I stroll along the dusty roads
Of our disappointing lives.
I want to understand the loads
Of precious lies in our archives.

I hardly know what I lived for,
My youth was cruelly hacked;
They drafted me into their war
To search for what they lacked.

Today, I hover much above
The dreamlands' ceiling
To resurrect the feeling
Of my never-ending love.

I am not afraid of the unknown,
My curiosity refused to fade,
As a questionable dice is thrown,
The concepts are well versed.
Only the future is unrehearsed.

I Looked for Dad

I looked for Dad,
Among the dead,
He wasn't there,
I looked elsewhere...

Escorted by my grieving,
I looked among the living
My father wasn't there,
It was agonizingly unfair.

The awful nightmares of those years
Were kept away from children's ears;
We weren't told about deaths and jails.
Only much later in my youth
After the gory war, they lifted a few veils,
I learned the ugly truth...

A brilliant young man was only twenty-nine,
They shot and threw his body into a mine;
And millions of others lost their lives,
Leaving behind their kids and wives.
If we forget Joe Stalin, the sadistic butcher,
These crimes will be repeated in the future.

We turn the other cheek,
They take us for the weak,
The bloody tyrants sell their souls,
We help them to attain their goals.

Don't ever guess,
I will respond if you insist:
I can't forget, I won't forgive
As long as gods may let me live.
Yes, yes and yes,
I want to hang each communist.

Hell Lived in Me

One year I lived quite well,
Hell lived in me those days;
I have received a lovely spell
From one who never prays,
From one who runs the world,
From one who knew the word.

Though, after he spent
Twelve moons with me,
He could not talk to anyone,
To those who whined and bent,
To those who are afraid and flee,
To those who've lied and gone,
To those who always borrow,
To those who on occasion lend,
To those who weep in sorrow,
To those who steal and spend.

A physical defeat
He turned into a moral
Victory for me:
He offered me a seat,
Made from a rosy coral
In his dominion of glee.

Last night,
The devil whispered
A pleasant thought
Into my eager ear,
"Nobody dies from love,
It is a mere poetic license
For those who see no light,
For those who dwell in fear."

At dawn,
I sowed sparkly glares,
At dusk,
I reaped new love affairs.

A Celebration of Suspense

I added flesh to bones,
Reshuffled a few verses,
They look like shallow clones,
Or tax collectors with no purses.

The world is in disarray,
A rug was pulled
From underneath the truth.
It's dark; our mood is blue 'n gray,
Our greed remains unruled,
Tomorrows don't invite our youth.

There are no guardrails
For us to hold
As we climb upstairs,
We even lost the mold
And cookie cutters for the heirs.

We keep them out of the fray,
Away from strain or troubles,
Occasionally, we even pray.
Why don't we pop the bubbles?

Something inside me
Won't disappear-
Won't go away.
I feel disasters tracking me.
I curb my fear,
But let my doubts stay.

A celebration of suspense
Inspires me and entertains
A page-turning curiosity.
I firmly pull the reins
And jump the fence
Between banality and virtuosity.

I Can't Embrace

I can't embrace
This nasty world,
I shape my base,
I hone my sword.

Eyes didn't reflect my past,
They missed another dawn;
Even eternity will never last
After my innocence is gone.

I'll rearrange the ancient map;
I'll ignore the calendar of lives;
I'll grasp the globe and wrap
It in the residue of our silly lies.

I'll harvest what I saw;
I'll march my extra mile;
I'll soar to see the glow,
I'll be triumphant in my trial.

I pledge to learn
When the fat lady sings;
I pledge to earn
A pair of angel's wings.

I Found My Old Album in the Attic

I found my old album in the attic;
Youthful smiles on dusty pages;
We're good-looking and romantic
Amongst some somber strangers.

It looked exactly what it was,
Burlesque of the wicked few.
It was a theatre and a pose,
But yet, it wasn't all we knew.

We knew the bullet's whistles,
We knew the deadly guns,
We were as innocent as crystals,
But daring as the empty drums.

Red-blooded boys, we play at war,
The bullets fly between our heads,
And bounce on a stony floor
Like needles with no threads.

I am turning brittle brown pages,
Our roots are buried in these photos;
Today, the souls of young avengers
Fly high above the roaring motors.

I crossed so many t's,
I sailed life's golden pond,
I know what dire war is
But miss that sacred bond.

The farewell photos of my past;
The actors struggle 'till they last;
The cozy play abruptly stopped,
The heartless curtain dropped.

I Entered Twice

I pounded the table,
But didn't climb the gable
Toward long-faltering desires,
At least, not yet.
I wouldn't break the ice,
I wouldn't change the set.
Life as a show must go on,
Long live, new dawn!
Farewell, sunset!

I entered twice
The river with no name,
It floats and veers
Between the good and vice,
Between obscurity and fame,
Between my foes and peers,
Between my honesty and lies,
Between my cries and laughter
Toward the final,
Yet unwritten chapter.

I heard:" Take heed,
For other side of silence
Will never need
A miracle of science
To reestablish paradigm
And justify the end of time."

Paul didn't accept my soul
Tormented and abused.
Peter rejected my sick body,
Gravely used.
They locked the gate to bliss.
I slid to the abyss.

I dropped the other shoe,
I crossed the line,
Went deeper.
I wish I knew,
That coffins made from pine
Are cheaper.

Horizon

Bad cards were dealt,
My life turns down South,
I plow up the Bible belt,
But seal my mouth.

I hear the sacred bell,
I try to stop the Earth,
I am sick of life in Hell,
I dream of my rebirth.

I put my meager wage
On what we really are:
On actors and the stage,
On hands caught in a jar,
On our greed and needs,
On our worthless deeds.

Dawn brings its dew
Into my gloomy day,
I sip my bitter brew,
I am in the final play.

I rise above my fear,
I drag my heavy cross;
Horizon, wait, for I am near,
I am your fearless albatross.

I bet, beyond that line
The grass is greener.
I hope behind that line
Even the air is cleaner.

I Chose a Gluttony Canteen

I am dating my nostalgic pain;
I am drunk; don't trust my plea:
I'll never write another song,
I'll never watch a flying crane,
Nobody hugs and kisses me,
I am just gadding all night long.

I hear
The old grandfather clock,
I hear
The never-ending chimes,
I hear
Somebody's anxious knock,
I hear
The metronome of times.

I'll invite my friends to dine,
No dieticians, no saboteurs;
I'll cook a five-course meal,
I'll serve my luscious wine,
I'll share my gastronomic zeal
With sybaritic connoisseurs.

I was quite hungry, often,
Until I learned to mask it;
I had to choose between
A broken pine-top coffin
And a bejeweled casket
Of our gluttony canteen.

I honestly prefer my wicked fun
Lit by a sentimental candlelight;
I disconnected our blazing sun
And chose the epicurean delight:
I simply cultivate my cozy dream,
Mushrooms de Paris a la Crème.

A Breezy Shade

Love doesn't conquer hate
As I believed for many years-
Neither good nor evil wait
To kill or heal our sticky fears.

An eye for an eye,
A life for a life.
There's no falling angel
In the sky,
Only a falling knife.

I turned two cheeks,
I couldn't fetch the third;
I'm surrounded by freaks,
Life's a theatre of absurd.

I'm too broke
To be too choosy,
I'm sitting on the grass
Wrapped in a breezy shade,
I've had my precious smoke,
I'm a little sad, a little woozy,
Time passes down my hourglass,
A monument of history we made.

I outlived my pension,
Old friends don't ever call-
I don't believe in my ascension,
I do believe in my inevitable fall.

We Tried to Love Somebody Else

We tried to love somebody else,
Someone besides ourselves,
As if we heard the church's bells
Inviting us upstairs.

We reaped what we have sowed,
We knew the cracks on every road,
Forgetting avenues and streets
That march to their bars and beats.

Easily forgiving duplicities of many,
But never individuality of one,
We wouldn't share even a penny
With one who's not like everyone.

We kill those whom we love,
Those who are strong, by sword;
Those who are weak, by kisses,
We choke them with an iron glove;
We mud them with the words
Amid self-adoration of Narcissus.

We listen to our friends and foes,
But hear the voices of ancestors
What tried to disconnect the dots.
We always stand upon our toes
To be above the common jesters,
And walk across the broken pots
Of our well forgotten love affairs,
Of loud circles morphed
Into the quiet squares.

Amnesia of Fate

Come into my sleep,
Enter my dream,
Please wake and stir
Creative treasures
That hide in the dark,
Find a door into the room
Of my regrets and doubts.
Please, bring the sun to
My wingless, wilted hope.

There are no pasts,
They die as humans,
As dawns and days,
As dusks and nights.
The sun of springs
Melts snows of winters.
Summers drown
In the rains of autumns,
Nostalgia erases our
Unpleasant memories.

I hear the cries of rain
Far above bloody fights;
I hear the voice of pain.
Those days and nights
Will never nip my heels,
I leave them
In the silent movie reels.

Amnesia of fate
Allows me to leave
The hordes of strangers
From my darker years.
Today,

I am waiting at the gate
To pass the final sieve.
Tomorrow,
I will wipe the angels'
Melancholic tears.

A Cross to Bear

Fast tires whizz by,
On wet highways they bounce.
The rainy skies,
The bubbles pounce,
Nobody chirps or flies,
A beaten autumn says goodbye.

Our souls are sold,
Hell is frozen,
St. Michael called,
The Lord is chosen.

I'm from another trinity,
A part of a ménage a trois.
Is it a beginning of infinity
Or just my last hurrah?

I have a cross to bear
I sow, thus I shall reap.
I'll be chastised for my affair,
I hope Hell isn't very deep.

I heard, all things must pass
And I'll find my greener grass.

The Countdown

Dogmatic axioms buried my pride,
And masked my unapologetic greed
As if my life's been a perpetual ride
Into a paradise always guaranteed.

I'm nervous, I'm a misfit,
I have no aura of stability,
Or peacefulness and wit,
I've lost my true invincibility.

I live not on what I chew,
But on what I digest.
I've been already blue,
Before my last arrest.

A cloud squeezed its juice
Onto a rustic and thirsty grass,
Young spring is on the loose,
But not allowed to trespass
Into the endless mausoleum.
I've never seen Him
But heard His words:
"Don't be stubbornly righteous,
Don't cheat yourself out of a life,
Be generally kind and good
Be good especially for someone."

It happened in a childhood,
The countdown has begun.

A Choice of Salt or Honey

One night of honey,
Brings days of pain.
I'm crying if it's sunny;
I'm dancing in the rain.

A few loud and feisty ravens
Will chase a red-tailed hawk,
Who flies into safe havens
For those who never walk.

An unexpected goodness
Gives purpose to my life.
I'm clueless whether
To be defeated or to strife.

A choice of salt or honey
Was given to my tired soul,
Amid my vanity and money,
I couldn't pick an easy stroll.

These lacy winter stars
Hang above frozen lakes
As memories and scars
And fragile snowflakes
Fall atop quiet slopes
As useless fading hopes.
.

They hurt my feelings.
I only wash my hands,
I often like beginnings,
But hate the happy ends.

A Gypsy Lady Holds My Hand

The line is drawn in the sand;
I'm looking for a quicker flow.
A gypsy lady holds my hand,
She'll foretell my fate and go.

There was no space to ramble,
Good fortunes easy to predict
Without an elaborate preamble,
My destiny was quickly picked:
"No one is strong enough
To break your tempered heart,
You'll say, goodbye, my love,
And load your cases on a cart."

The knife of our sad farewell
Carved "love you" on a bench.
Life turned into a hollow shell,
Forgotten in a muddy trench.
The gypsy lied.
My broken heart
Still bleeds
Till death us part.

We left our mothers' wombs
To walk through hell of glee,
As if we never had enough.
My daily melancholy looms,
I'm still a detainee of love,
That gypsy lady got her fee.

The cotton balls of guilty clouds
Descending on the lifeless trees,
I'm already wrapped in shrouds,
Expecting the abyss to freeze.

All-Forgiving Death

The vaudevilles of life
Play over intermission,
Our ghastly daily strife
Neared its completion.

We are still blind-
We are still deaf-
We are resigned
To all-forgiving death.

As wise men used to say,
"Stop and smell the roses,
Love comes to us to play
As a reality without poses.
We are the actors
On the stage of life;
We hustle on its hectares,
In our never-ending strife."

Left over by the moon,
The river ebbs at noon,
The sun is on its way
Behind the golden trees,
If this is not a happy day,
What is?

A Beast Four-Footed

My hectic past was looted,
My future seems too dark,
I'm like a beast four-footed
Under a tender rainbow arc.

I sail my bottle-ship,
And slowly drown
In a sea of wine.
Some gulp, I try to sip,
Some say I'm a clown,
Some say I'm a swine.

My bottle-ship is sealed,
A life not of my choosing,
Somewhere inside I build
A visceral hate of boozing.

It's a first date,
We're wearing our masks,
Mine mourns, hers winks.
It's somewhat late,
But the bartender asks,
Whether we like the drinks.

We only spend a single day
In a bliss of love and grace;
She awakes and runs away,
And leaves no name to trace.

I'm still vigorously dating,
To dock my homeless heart,
And get the highest rating.
I'm naïve. They're very smart.

A Life Devoured

A little fish wakes up and flaunts
Her luminescent, precious scales,
Upsetting self-complacent ripples,
Tenderly caressed by early dawn.
The sun will push the haze aside
A new day wraps us in its pleasures.

I am journeying on a pair of rails,
Coldblooded, pasty, never-ending,
Surrounded by squeaky sounds
Of an impatient train usurping me
Towards the certainty of a lifeless,
Yet ominous, joy-crashing curtain
And the stability of irritating pain
Artfully hiding in my last farewell
To a life devoured by my eternal
Admiration.

At dawn, I stroll along the Milky Way
On my dilapidated feet of clay,
But am distracted
By a shiny penny
Tossed into the air.
Life is a stage; I humbly act;
There are few other roles, if any,
I cannot choose, I wouldn't dare.
The genie leaves the bottle
Without even asking what I want.
I am not Einstein or Aristotle,
I am just a lifelong debutant.
Moreover, I am not a throttle,
I wouldn't choke the show,
I sing the only song I know.

I Am In You

My watch has stopped.
A red cardinal knocked on the window and woke me up.
Still dark; I hear the whisper of your breath.
Your skin has the drunken scent of honey.
Daylight snuck into our room between the blinds
And painted hazy wavy stripes on us.
The velvet of your skin,
The scent of honeydew,
Your tender sleepy grin,
My only blissful avenue.
Our personal stairway to promised heaven,
My copper-withered lips touched your silky cheek,
Your neck, your shoulder and a breast.
I want to wake you up with my thirsty kisses.
You're slowly opening your eyes;
You smile and break the silence with a purr of pleasure.
My hands are wandering all over your body,
Like two longing, hungry hounds.
You touch and kiss me.
We hug and drink each other's kisses.
I am in you. We're swimming in carnal pleasure,
In an unrestricted ocean of ecstasy.
We're two hearts that beat as one.
We drown.
My watch has stopped.
Long live a little death!

No One Can Circle Squares

I lived a life unbound,
Without rules and trends,
But only in the final round
I recognized my enemies
Disguised as friends.

No one can circle squares
And make the corners disappear,
No one can climb the stairs
Of someone else's bright career.

The deck is being shuffled,
Let's play a prehistoric game,
Let's climb that golden scaffold
Let's build the Tower of Babel,
Life's just a game of Scrabble,
The highs 'n lows are the same.

As my beloved Heracles,
I cleaned the Augean stables,
The cattle tossed few miracles
To animate the Aesop's fables.
I shook the tree of knowledge
And watched, but nothing fell,
No thoughts, no fruits…
I didn't go to a private college,
I looked, but missed the well
Where wisdom takes its roots.

Between the Moonlit Walls

Devoured stars
Become black holes,
Such splendors of the skies.
Because behind the bars,
Between the moonlit walls
The sun will never rise.

My life is a gleaming bluff
Of undeserved superiority
As if I'm in sole possession
Of all four aces in my cuff.
No sense of meek inferiority,
No darkness of depression.

I lured devotion of élan
From those who knew me well,
I even knew what's going on
When Jesus went to Hell.
I saw when he returned
To Magdalene,
I watched their hugs and kisses;
It was the most amazing scene
Of God and his beloved mistress.

Perpetually flowing crowds,
Occasionally pouring rains.
Dispersed my heavy doubts,
But only happiness remains.

Along with Aesthetic Deafness

I'm mulling at this time,
Over my life's illusive paradigm;
I ask myself from time to time,
Have I forgotten more
Than some will ever know?
Am I already at the door
That separates my life
From death's perpetual glow?

My mind is a peculiar place
Where new ideas meet at night
To check the curiosity of intellects
Along with their aesthetic deafness.
A place where good and evil fight,
The two most unforgiving sects,
Both passionate and selfless.

The golden glow of autumn grieves,
And strokes old salt-wrinkled faces
Of my surviving wartime peers.
On their nostalgic bases,
Loaded with bravery and fears,
Amid the memories of fallen leaves.

The quilt of a red-headed autumn
Rests on the rusty branches
And waits for the frosty days.
As if a yet unknown quantum
Inside the snowy avalanches
Still longs for the sunny rays.

I'm mulling, at this time,
Over my life's illusive paradigm.
My pies are crowding the skies

Above the land, above the seas,
Over the golden, honeyed shore.
My angel didn't dot the i's,
My savior didn't cross the t's,
He went to fight the final war
Of virtues, with my endless sins.

A Fallen Angel Waited

A boat won't sail the seas
Until it leaves its berth;
One can't rejoice in bliss
Until he cried on Earth.

I wouldn't want to vie
If she decides to leave,
I'll groan out a goodbye,
Then honestly forgive.
She'll leave; I'll grieve-
I'll unfurl my wings and fly.

A rationale abated
In my corroded youth,
I tried to do my best.
A fallen angel waited
To learn the final truth.
He noosed the rope,
Yet granted my request
He gave away a clue,
"The bird of hope
Was never blue."

The sun scorched my street,
The sky turned upside-down
Over the arcs of rainbows.
My future wears a crown
And walks on two bare feet.
The rivers flip their flows
Into the tides of a holy sea,
Reflecting irritated skies,
They're innocent and free
To fade into the red sunrise.

I hear my tired-out heart,
I'm marching to its beat,
I morph into a work of art.
I'm the maven of my street.
Attracted to a crafty lure
A fallen angel waiting,
He begs me for the cure
From self-inflicted hating.

Have Faith in Science

I asked my Lord,
To break his silence,
Here is his word:
"Have faith in science,
I'll tear your rope,
I'll set you free,
I'll give you hope,
I'll let you be..."

I close my eyes,
Mirages shimmer,
I cross my fingers
And toss the dice;
I'm still a dreamer,
My hope still lingers.

I asked my past
To make me smart,
I learned, at last,
Life is a dying art.

The fittest run the world,
No mercy for the weak,
A doctor cuts the cord
Through thin or thick.

I am alone, I really learn
To steal or work and earn,
To fight and hate or love,
To be a worm or fly above.

Don't trust the elders,
Have faith in science,
Scratch a few fenders,
Enjoy a wise defiance.

A Casual Bloodbath

A casual bloodbath,
Just a new day at war,
No peace in wrath,
We locked that door.

Don't waste your word-
She won't be back.
Don't raise your sword,
Just run your lonely track.

Avengers never seek
A peaceful resistance,
There is no other cheek,
Just a lifelong distance.

We often hide our love
Under the guise of hate.
Be first if life is deep enough,
But then, it's somewhat late.

Lovers have expiration dates,
But no one reads the tags.
We only recognize their fates
When we obtain their body bags.

Love can't return.
A star of each romance
Falls from the skies.
We never try to learn,
We're afraid to take a chance
And leave this puzzling paradise.

A Child That Never Had Enough

A poet sees himself only
As someone iniquitous,
Nevertheless, a teacher,
Always ubiquitous,
Nevertheless, a preacher
Before the friends, yet lonely.

Life is the darkest
Before it is wholly black,
My falls are hardest,
Before the ending wrack.

Life knows wicked ways
To skin a cat.
It dumps on me few lucky days
And I'm left flaunting my top hat,
It's suddenly a vortex; I dive
Into my misery from eight to five.

Life is a song I haven't sung,
I only whispered words of love.
It is a spring that has not sprung;
It is a child that never had enough.

While Saturn was devouring
His children,
The ghost of destiny,
Enthusiastic and esteemed,
Went to a graveyard
And carved a golden epitaph
On my tombstone,
"He lived the way he dreamed-
Alone".

A Confession

I'm an oyster in the desert,
I'm a lobster climbing hills,
Life is my unwanted present,
Nevertheless, I pay my bills.

I'm just a shattered vase,
I'm a mastermind of plots,
I'm a labyrinth; I'm a maze,
I'm splitting my verbal hair
I'm a futile god of polyglots,
I'm a barker at a country fair.

Please, don't invite me back.
My dark desires are twisted,
I'm not a member of the pack
Among the heavily fisted.

I love these careless days
I'm a self-admiring amateur
Who sings Amazing Grace;
I'm a graveyard connoisseur.

I never chase the ambulance,
I tightly hold my brazen horses,
I only exercise my abstinence,
I publish my unpolished verses.

Entropy

I am Casanova unemployed;
I morph into a social misfit.
I am a self-defeating Freud,
Resenting my sarcastic wit.

I turn an arrhythmia of hearts
Into the rhythms of verses,
As old pedantic paradigm
Into confusions of the arts,
Into decaffeinated sermons,
Into a puzzling pantomime,
Into an organized disorder
Of our basic brick and mortar.

I turn a prudent compromise
Between eternal subjectivity
And a magnificent sunrise
Jostling its way into longevity.

I'm dazed and confused,
The night is not too light,
Too dark were all the others.
The moon is uttering tonight,
A blinding darkness fuses
My working girls with hordes
Of patiently cheating fathers.

The more I know,
The less I sleep,
The more I sow,
The less I reap.

I Grab the Falling Knives

I grab the falling knives
To save some helpless lives,
And noose the ends of ropes
To hang their fragile hopes.

I try to save my face
And yet, I walk my days
The same old route:
I'm in debt, I'm in doubt.

The envelope was sealed.
Nobody saved the world,
The future has been willed
To one who knew the word.

My cover has been blown,
Bliss ends where it begins.
The quilt was quickly sewn
To mask my mortal sins.

Don't hurt me when I laugh,
There's a better side of me.
I always show just a half,
The rest you'll never see;
I'll never show you my pain,
That side is dark and vain.

I long for dawn
After my back-to-back
Sunsets.
I'm a wingless swan,
I'm left alone
To place my losing bets.
Over the same old route,
I'm in debt, I'm in doubt.

Downhill to Dwell

I take these seven
With a grain of salt,
Greed, envy, pride and lust,
Gluttony, wrath and sloth.
I'm chugging through this dust
Toward a promised heaven,
Where doctors give their oath,
While angels turn a somersault.
Safeguarding our moral values
At the doorsteps of the abyss.
He needs a fodder for his rallies,
For us it is a final Judas' kiss.

Life is an interest-free loan,
For some, it's a free lunch,
Even a gallant, black-tie dinner.
These deals are set in stone.
If you decide to be a winner,
Try not to live by bread alone.

Exquisite books are waiting
On my desk
To share with me their filigree
Of knowledge,
Like harmony of the grotesque
Deliver science into carnage.

I loathe all pros and cons,
Their uninspired platitudes,
Polluting modern lexicons
Of so-called bros and dudes.

In a hot, crowded dungeon,
I see my devil in the flesh,
Long horns, feet to the fire.
He has a gourmet luncheon,
Potatoes with creme freiche
And frogs from a quagmire.

Whether it is bliss or Hell,
I'm fated downhill to dwell.

At Night

Astrology of our stars,
Eternity of our essence,
Hysteria of our decay,
Pathology of our scars,
Infinity of our presence
Dwell in the Milky Way.

I am alone in my cold bed
And cannot close my eyes.
My demons come at night,
To make the sunsets red.
My startled teardrop dries
Before the morning light.

I cultivate inside me
Desires to break away,
And live in a daily glee,
At times, above the fray.

A man is made from clay;
Same goes for the rest.
I know, I'm an old sage,
Always a predator or prey.
This night, I did my best,
I locked my golden cage.

Don't toy with my old pain,
Your sugar hurts my teeth,
I slowly circle in the drain,
Like an old wedding wreath.

The gift of intellect
Subdues the flashes
Of my eternal doubt.
After I die, I do elect
Just humble ashes
As a reward for being
Vain and proud.

At Eighty-three

The Mount of Ascension,
The Rock of Agony,
The Gethsemane,
I walk the fourth dimension,
I walk the fragile harmony
Along the memories of pain.

At eighty-three,
I have a shorter list '
Of victories to chase.
I ask," To be or not to be?"
Then touch my wrist
To check the pulse,
"Well, just in case."

I've never seen
A perfect good or evil,
The truth is in between
As long as we are civil
And wine is dry and clean.

Good must have bullets
To survive,
But evil doesn't need the guns.
The lovely couple will forever
Thrive,
Like stubborn fathers,
Like nihilistic sons.

The line is drawn
Across a life of shame,
The days are numbly somber.
The camouflage is blown
Off lives that passed the blame.
I was a man: I became a number
And went to bed.
Thank God the dogs are fed.

Burned with the sun,
I won't enjoy the lights,
Don't wake me up to run
Toward the endless fights,
Please, let me sleep,
I sow, but hate to reap.

As if We Never Parted

My savior saints got lost
Between the leaded clouds;
I want them back at any cost
To cure my self-inflicted doubts.

My life was just a habit,
A prearranged routine,
I paid in full my hefty debit
For someone else's unforgiven sin.

Don't start your timeworn game:
I came to see you from the past,
To love again without any blame.
I'm a romantic man, a boy no more.
The years of youth don't ever last,
Only first loves refuse to cease,
I pleaded yet again: open the door;
I tearfully begged you on my knees.

It seems as if we never met,
It seems as if we never parted.
Regrettably, you placed your bet,
And the old games have started.

We paced between the naked trees,
Over a tender blanket of the snow,
We left behind the deep footprints
Of our tenebrous but yearning show.

A Bugle Playing

I hate to argue with this cretin,
He thinks the same of me,
Only our morbid egos threaten
To reach the promised glee.

Forget the ins and outs
Of our Apostles' creed,
The only truths and doubts
Are those fossils that still bleed.

Life is pain.
In vain, I push it to the limit,
Do I deserve to win it?
I am happy as a picnic basket
Until my dreams collapse,
Until I hear above my casket
A bugle playing farewell taps
To recollect, not to complain.

My train has drifted
And finally derailed.
It slid into a cul de sac,
Far from the morals scripted.
The Book as always failed
To put me on a lighter track.

My gun is waiting
For the final draw--
I am still debating
Whether it is my flaw.

I Left Naiveté Behind

I've seen that movie once,
I squeezed that lemon,
I ate that bitter sandwich.
Today, I changed my mind;
Today, I can pronounce
Sweet nectar or dire venom,
I learned their language,
I left naiveté behind.

So garrulous and stupid,
A cupid sent two darts,
He was a vicious cupid,
He pierced our hearts.

Brash and erotic passions
Broke vulnerable limbs
From trees of our emotions,
And blinded our eyes;
We laid our bets on dreams,
I'm left to pay the price.

I have no friends to love,
I am playing chess alone,
Maybe I am not bad enough,
For Satan to create my clone.

I learned the primal word,
I saw the mighty blinding rod;
We were created by a sword
In hands of Lucifer, not God.

When my poor soul arrives
To see a god of lightning and thunder,
He'll let me choose between two lives;
I chose the one which is above,
But not the one that's six feet under.

I Clothed You with a Rain

I was a boy, half-crazed,
You knew I was insane,
My eyes were glazed,
I clothed you with a rain
And fell in love with you,
You didn't have a clue.

You wore a silky gown
Made of the rainy skies,
The autumn drowned
In your inviting eyes.

You were my dawn,
A vivid rainbow arc;
Today, you've gone,
The skies are stark.

The truth was spoken,
We couldn't hold our rage,
Our hearts were broken
And left their golden cage.

Life took a friendless walk
Along the naked trees,
Dusted by a snowy chalk
And patted by the breeze.

A guiltless tender dream
Ascended empty-handed,
Nobody heard my scream.

The night descended.

Emotional Intelligence

Too many problems on my plate,
It looks like yet another civil war.
I found those who'd bite the bait,
And those who'd crawl or soar.

There are no stars of hope
Above a super sentimental fudge,
There is a steep and sloppy slope
Into a jingoistic grudge.

Emotional intelligence,
Intelligent emotions.
What's in the word?
Tuxedo-flaunting gents
Or ladies soaked in lotions;
No one can save the world,
Except a psychological defiance
Of realistic common sense,
Except a collective guilty silence
About the bliss beyond the fence.

Souls dressed in army camouflage
Are dumped from the meat wagons,
With medals on their swollen chests.
Few stoic mothers in the entourage
Saw wars as fire-breathing dragons,
They heard death's horrid mocking,
"Boys' lives deserved their rests."

I crane my neck
To see tomorrows,
There is a wreck
Of weeping sorrows.

I Am a Wolf

I am a wolf,
I'm forced to be a dog;
I can be what I'm not,
But only for a while.
I am still alive
By virtue of my strength
And prowess,
Without countless
Sit, stay and heel,
Then begging for a meal.

There is another world
Beyond my safety blanket.
There is a glitzy banquet
To honor my predatory day;
Only at night I am a prey.

There is another world
Beyond my comfort zone,
I see the sun is climbing
To its zenith room,
Or maybe it is I'm sliding
Into my gloom,
Or yet, that's the unknown
That badly needs the word;
Where is the Lord?

What's fair or what is not?
Somebody's trash
Is someone else's treasure;
Even the Gordian knot
Was only Alexander's
Shrewdness' measure.

I am a wolf,
I am just forced to be a dog;
My vigilance is not required
To live and later to be saved;
I wait remorsefully quiet,
My way to heaven isn't paved.

A Cup of English Tea

I built for us this castle
On a sunsets' hiding hill,
Days pass much faster,
If they will not, I will.

A dull and tedious rerun-
A cup of English tea
Marks five o'clock;
A slice of lemon
Glistens like the sun
Returning to the sea,
To drown like a rock
Or swim like salmon.

I didn't return from war,
I brought it back with me;
You met me at the door,
I wore a mask of glee.

Gray clouds
Swimming in a river
Like dusty shrouds
From an ancient grave.
I rarely take; I'm a giver;
I never dig, I only pave.
I'm a disobedient dog,
I'm trained, yet rogue.

You didn't try to love me,
Your heart will never fly
Toward sugarcoated glee,
Toward a castle in the sky.

If that's your preference,
You're free to go;
Without a tear or sorrow,
It's common sense,
Let's dance our final tango
And split at dawn tomorrow.

I Took a Redeye Flight

I took a redeye flight
And came to church
To see the light.
A scarlet letter "L",
Which stood for "Lost",
Was glued to my lapel.
The Holy Spirit
Didn't have to search
For me at Pentecost.

My life reminds me
Of a great romance;
My last romance
Do not resemble life.

A short goodbye,
We hugged and kissed
Nothing was left unsaid;
Our future slashed its wrist,
But only the sunset bled.

I missed green lights of hope,
I saw red lights of a dispair,
I even saw tomorrows
Through the scope.
There were no luring lights,
There were only sorrows;
I'd rather land elsewhere.

Angry Man

Life never deals
A pair of aces
With four Jacks.
It always feels
I lost my races
To the hacks.

The slope is shallow,
But I am shovel-ready.
I hardly cast a shadow,
Only my mind is steady.

My fate is sealed
Even before I swoon
Under a dire torture.
I plot to run across a field,
But not a day too soon,
I'm a tired soldier of fortune.

My friends unkindly say,
That no one waits for me
Behind the prison wall.
I'll be unchained someday,
I'll hunt, my foes will flee,
But some heads have to fall.

I seldom see the lights
Behind my dark cell's bars,
I curse the dreamy nights,
But crave the blinking stars.

Those days have passed,
Nobody needs my anger,
I'm just an aged pushover,
I have deserved my rest.
And like a retired ganger,
I chew the lifeless clover.

There are no prison bars,
There are no shiny stars,
Only a few lackluster lights,
And brutal sleepless nights.

Fate

I'm puzzled with the afterlives
Of those who bought the farms.
They strived, but lost their drives,
Their clocks won't need the arms.

Their souls don't speak to me,
Abandoned like the wrecks
Of riches disappeared at sea.
The deal was carved in stone,
Fate chained it to their necks.
My fate was kind, I am alone.

I rest under the shady trees
They're thoughtfully planted.
I reap the fruits of bliss
And take them all for granted.
Fate knew the scrolls unfurled,
But failed to trust a single one.
While the dead souls swirled,
Until there were none.
I squandered precious time,
While fate turned on a dime.

Our history was written
By the winners,
Adjusted by the smitten,
Injected with self-serving lies,
Then ironed by the spinners,
Neglecting our muted cries.

Enigma of the Future's Past

A quiet morning, autumn's gold,
The hues of honey on the floor,
I reckon what my mother told,
"Keep the unknown at the door."

This is a trying time;
I slide into the ominous abyss,
Numb as a speechless mime,
Cold as a lackluster kiss.

A man is either predator or prey-
His heart is made of steel or clay.

The blades of fire,
The haze of smoke,
The scene was dire,
I went for broke.

Our nature's feeding breast
Is much kinder than it seems;
I soar into the light of grace
Above the mountain crest.
I look for a hollowed place,
A cradle of my cozy dreams.

An enigma of the future's past
Rocks gently on the waves;
I see the smiling sun, at last,
That lights our silent graves.

The night dawned sun onto my face,
And waves of an angry river roared;
I walked my strong-willed life to graze,
Across the shallow waters of the ford.

Evangelists of Lies

You're a gracious swan;
You're a forbidden fruit,
Not very ripe, but willing.
You're the greener grass;
I'm dusk, you're still dawn,
You're a lady, I'm a brute-
I'm an empty glass;
I need refilling.

A mask that you so often wear
Shows the sorrow in your eyes.
The silky river of your hair
Floats innocence and lies.

You sizzle on my pan,
As we make love,
I'm that lucky man
Who called your bluff.

I'll doubt you,
And won't believe myself;
I'd hate to plow through
Those trusted twelve.

You'll cheat on him,
You'll cheat on me,
I've seen that film
Two times or three.

Evangelists of lies,
I am so glad, you've gone,
In Hell or in the skies
You'll never see the sun.

Tonight,
You're dancing on the table;
King Herod has to pay.
I learned too well this fable,
My head is on that tray.

Eternal Tango

She is a nightclub striptease dancer,
Undressed like forests in the winter.
I am a ruthless tattooed bouncer,
A sentimental brute, a loner-drifter.

Let's put ourselves to work,
Put on your dancing shoes;
I'll lead you to the road's fork.
What's next? You choose.

Just follow my right palm;
Make your enticing moves.
Use your disarming charm
Along the tango grooves.

We'll dance our way
Between the tables
Into a happy day
From our grim fables.

Two souls, one pain;
Two loves, one ploy;
Two lines, one lane
Into our endless joy.

The tango of two doves,
The harbor of two loves,
The tango of two lives
Into eternal paradise.

Ethereal Wisdom

The less I dig,
The speedier I fall.
I have to choose
A smaller part of something big,
But if I lose,
A bigger part of something small.

Life is a merciless school,
It's just another trusted liar
That's turning on a dime.
One learns unless he's a fool,
The other aims much higher,
He wants Mount Everest to climb,
Or possibly the stairway of worry,
And fly as Icarus to death and glory.

Foes always cheer,
Friends often leave
And all the pieces of the puzzle
Will fall into their grooves.
The highest priest will slyly veer
And ask us to believe
In myths or razzle-dazzle
Of lives above the hooves.

My whisper
Morphs into a scream
Obscurely sinister,
Just like a morbid dream.
I am an autumn leaf;
Life is a dying branch,
So painfully and vainly brief,
God's venomous revenge.

A sharp-eyed verse
Foresaw my future
Years ahead,
Piercing my days and nights
As if it were a vicious curse,
As if it were a sturdy suture
Joining my farewell sunset
With promised everlasting lights.

Etude

Love warms my face,
Love burns my heart;
Love, you're wrapped in lace;
Love, I'm your steadfast bard.

I find diamonds in the rough,
And roses in the thorny brier.
I often soar into my loves
Like butterflies into a fire.

This love was earned,
She knew the price.
My wings were burned,
She threw the ice.

I travel through the world;
In my rose-colored glasses.
I lease my room and board
In Paris, on Montparnasse,
An opioid for the masses.
The hill for mediocre artists,
The hill for expert lovers,
The hill for fancy parties,
A textbook with no covers.

It is my dorm,
But not my wife,
My bed is warm,
I love this life!

Hey, Cabby

Hey, cabby,
We are close enough,
I have no place to go
Or let it be;
I have no one to love
Besides the traffic flow.

Time has arrived
To make a choice,
To hear my voice,
To choose a side
Among the ploys;
I'm still mortified.

The connoisseurs are sorry,
A book of history is clueless
Before the tallest wall of worry.
Whether you're Helen of Troy
In front of olden gates to glory
Or a worn-out goddess Venus.
You cross the threshold in a hurry
Then ambushed in a vicious ploy.

I hear my inner voices,
About my two choices-
"Get busy living,
Get busy dying."
I've chosen leaving,
Why am I crying?

I had enough; no place to hide,
I have no one to love, I tried;
Hey, cabby, please, don't park
Until you see the heaven's arc.

Faustian Pact

I clean the Augean stables
From miles of nervous rhymes,
From metaphoric Aesop's fables,
From punishment without crimes.

In spite of our sworn allegiance
To common perfect orders,
To universal paradigm,
We act like greedy pigeons
With personality disorders
That turn our pledges on a dime.

No parties last forever
Within obscurities and newness,
No one is always wise and clever
Even in a vast and total trueness.

Today, I'm not fearful of anything,
After a life of the abandoned few,
A life as brutal as a boxing ring,
A life that even my angel overflew.

At night, I heard a distant toll
And signed the Faustian pact.
The devil bought my soul,
A basic upfront quid pro quo.
The deck was never stacked.
The devil lost. I'm in the know.

Applauds and vivid flowers
Pour honey on my heart.
I climb the totem pole
Between the darkest hours,
When my tomorrow falls apart,
And vanishes in a pigeonhole.

Farewell, my Gallant Matador

The squeaky trunks of trees
Sway slowly in a scorching wind,
The sun is hiding in the leaves
Like a teen-ager who has sinned.

The spiders weave their lace,
Long branches scratch the sky
Unruly twigs try to embrace,
It's hot, even the birds don't fly.

I'm in Barcelona, Spain.,
I watch the Catalonian night.
I watch the opulence of pain;
I watch the last bullfight.
I watch the matadors jaywalk;
I watch a bloody, shaken bull;
I listen to a heartless squawk,
I hold a drink; my glass is full.

Dusk pulls the sun away,
No one can save the day.
The sky is burning,
The southern night
Without a warning,
Turns off the light.

Farewell, my gallant matador,
A merciless mockery no more.
Farewell to that majestic bull,
Which kept my wineglass full.

A Day is Just An Exhibition

Nostalgia may trigger
A timely ruthless blast
Into a lackluster vigor
Of our cheerless past.

Life is a translucent candy
Wrapped in opaque illusions,
Dressed like a glitzy dandy
Protected from collusions.

The nights of anonymity
And uncontained emotions,
Calmly develop our affinity
For indefensible devotions.

Maturity will nearly shatter
Our younger frigid image,
We'll write another chapter
Of our fruitless scrimmage.

Rehearsals for the players
Will help to keep the score,
We daily peel these layers,
Before we reach the core.

A day is just an exhibition,
Only a tiny piece of truth,
Life is a lethal competition
Of our death and youth.

The Crisp Boneyards

What's life? No one yet knows,
Life comes from yesterdays,
And veers between tomorrows,
It seldom leaves a trace.

The crisp boneyards
Of weary summers
That alter into falls,
Become postcards
Of yellow, blue and red.
While quiet mourners
Tearfully stroll
Between the dead.

I'm at the threshold
Of a splendid life,
Though most foretold
I'll win this strife.
Those wishes lasted
Until they faded;
I firmly trusted
That life is gold.
Whether I hold or fold,
It's slightly overrated.

Even in our metric age,
I'm about six feet tall,
I'm not acting on the stage,
Life's no longer a masked ball.

And Visions Passed Away

I won't denounce dawn's
Invitation to a day,
Nor dusk's creation of a night.
The darkness makes us gray,
Thus, I'm longing for daylight.

Days throw tunes into my soul,
And weave new songs' bouquets,
At nights, stars fall into my sleep,
Past my rose-colored glasses.
I'm a common con man on parole
Mumbling my dining table's grace,
But have no time to sigh or weep
Like elders taking yoga classes.

It took me eighty years
Since birth,
To visit enigmatic corners
Of the Earth;
I saw my guiltlessness and sins,
I lost some everlasting fears
In waterfalls and vicious burners.
I learned the sacramental truth,
I missed the carelessness of youth.

I heard a voice:
"I'll put a yoke of arrogance on you,
I'll take compassion from your heart,
I promise, you'll never have a clue
That birth and death don't live apart."

These problems kept me in the dark,
I could no longer see the light of day.
I didn't get an invitation to Noah's ark
And my ecstatic visions passed away.

An Exit Sentence

The smoke of cigarettes
Is as nostalgic dreams
It floats and slowly melts
Amid the sun's hot beams.

The roads of rosy hopes
Adorned by weeping willows,
Run like the endless ropes
Into a world no one yet knows.

There's a door in every wall
That I impatiently try to find,
There's a pain in every soul
And its panacea intertwined.

I live a life I didn't earn,
The giver asked me
Nothing in return.
Life was bestowed on me.
Today, my birth certificate
Becomes an exit sentence,
Though life's quite intricate
And superficially relentless.

I saw the end of weary days,
I didn't have to cast the dice
To win the happy walkways
Of yet unknown paradise.

Down the River

Equations lend themselves
To boredom,
And mediocrity's lackluster,
While talents soar above
The Brunelleschi Dome,
Below God's quaint filibuster.

I glue new layers of veneer
To cover weary roughness
Of my misogynistic bouts.
I entertain back-biting fear
Of modern ladies' toughness
And quagmire of their doubts.

I sent my soul down the river,
It disappeared under the flow;
My angel honed his cleaver,
I'm ready for its ending blow.
God's fairness lost my trust,
I'd rather turn my face to evil,
Believe me, I'll do it, if I must.

There's no sun without you,
Life is a loveless marathon,
Come back, don't stay away,
I beg you for a single dawn.
I promise, I'll earn your love
Before a misty morning dew,
Before the tears of a new day.

I caught more flies with honey,
I even sliced the Gordian knot,
And yet, despite some doubts,
I saw the skies were sunny,
Whether I'm loved or not
Above the leaded clouds.

George Heard my Prayer

The music of a train,
The silence of a sail,
The frozen tears of rain,
The noisy beans of hail,
Even the cries of pain
Come as the daily mail.

My nerves were frayed.
I made my meek attempt
To be myself. I was afraid
Of yet another sacrament.

I saw them in my dreams,
Those blissful tomorrows
Without ghastly screams,
Without dreadful sorrows.

I huffed and spun away,
I tried to figure out how
To live in a befallen day,
To conquer what is now.

My nerves were frayed-
I knelt and calmly prayed.
I saw The Dragon Slayer.
George heard my prayer.

Good and Evil

I heard a scorching cry,
Another angel left the sky,
Fell from the light of bliss
Into the depth of the abyss.

War marked me with the scars;
I used to wear those souvenirs
Then brought them to the stars,
To puzzling new frontiers
Along the boundaries of grace,
To heal them in divine embrace.

I often sow the seeds of vines-
I hope my life is still quite fertile,
Then reap the sacred signs
To keep my soul immortal.

Eternity of good and evil
Unites pervasive powers
Into a never-ending river
Of our daily quid pro quo;
We bid goodbye for a hello.

At dusk,
I speak to gods for ours;
At dawn,
The fallen angel sends me
Flowers.

Give Us a Happy Hour

Star-studded Milky Way,
Please, kiss goodbye our
Ever-changing world.
Give us a happy hour,
Please, cut the futile cord,
Send our planet far away.

Some have too much,
They guzzle caviar for lunch.
Some bring a silver tray
And pawn their treasures.
Some only fly above the fray
And entertain their pleasures.

When God declares his verdict,
We calmly climb the guillotine.
Only a fallen angel can predict
Our fate as headless or pristine.

I outlived my guilt and sorrow.
If I need heart, I simply borrow.
I'm alive and teeter on the brink
Of yet another thoughtless war,
I really need another hefty drink.

Life's like a church, I'm its whore-
I try to get some paint or ink
To write on a revolving door:
"Enough, No More,
Make Love, Not War!"

Give me Your Heart

I write my half-baked memoirs;
I listen to no one in churches;
I hear the whisper of the stars,
I listen to the leaves on birches.

I wouldn't worship in the shrines-
I learned to live under a curfew.
I tried to read between the lines,
I combed the globe to find you.

When rivers run,
There is no end,
The sinking sun
Will not ascend.

Here's your wedding band,
Brought on a cupid's dart
Wear and enjoy this art.
Please, take my hand,
Give me your heart.

I'll listen to the strings of rain,
I'll erase the memories of pain,
And diamonds of morning dew
Will see my happy life with you.

Gertrude's Roses

Aesthetic discipline of literary metrics,
Refinement of our poetic fathers,
Artistic trampoline of bold eccentrics,
Are barricades for my erratic brothers.

In the pursuit of hefty purses
They canceled rhymes in verses,
Yet truly gifted poets of the world
Still chisel every letter in a word.

The genesis of my strong beliefs
Depicted in the ancient bas-reliefs.
Just hold your horses and take five,
Smell Gertrude's roses, get a life.

Futile Errands

I didn't choose my parents;
I didn't choose my motherland;
I wasted youth on running futile
Errands
For those whose checks were
In the mail
And those with cash in hands.

I etched in memories of grief,
My foolish oaths and pledges,
Like a rehabilitated thief
Scorched at the edges.

Don't let me leave the crowd-
Don't let me be a leader.
Don't paddle my canoe.
At times, I'm vain and proud,
But I'm not their feeder,
Don't let them dip their ladles
In my stew.

Three wise men veer
Between the crumbling dunes
Like sailboats along the tides.,
I feverously follow them
Sipping my ice-cold beer,
Ears plugged with jazzy tunes,
Avoiding narrative of guides
Under the Star of Bethlehem.

Gods dropped a final curtain
Over my fragile fate
With their almighty blow.
I'm absolutely certain,
Glee is reflecting in my plate
And I'm basking in its glow.

Friday Night

I can't acquire my glee again,
Limelight is a great pretender.
Small talks with a bartender
And a cute cocktail waitress,
Both frivolous and brainless.

Some young and pretty,
Some old and wrinkled,
Well-mannered hookers
Flaunt their merchandise
Wrapped in deodorants.

The ice cubes' crackling
Dilute our precious drinks.
I take my "Maker's Mark"
As always neat
In a warm snifter,
I haven't lost the beat.

Sharp loud voices
From the billiard tables
Attract red-blooded men
To try their luck.
I played a game of snookers
And won a hundred bucks.
While a few lovely hookers,
Lined at the wall like ducks.

Routinely crawling Friday night
For those who hope to drown
Their isolation in the crowd
Of a happy hour limelight.

I have no skin in daily games-
I'm thinking in long terms.
I have a set of luscious aims,
I place my bets on the interns.

First Dance

Two swans enjoy their regal glide
Reflected in the mirror of the lake.
First dance. The groom and bride.
I hope they'll be happy in the wake.

Their ecstasy soars in the skies,
Their sorrow slides into the valley,
The lake rocks sighs and smiles,
Surreal like in the works of Dali.

Two figures on the wedding cake,
Two dancers over the Swan Lake,
A trembling bride follows her fate,
A groom wants to undress a mate.

The devil's apple bite
Brings doubts unto a bride,
A groom enjoys the night,
No wisdom, only pride.

Among decisions of the mind
And intuitions of the heart,
The blind will lead the blind
Until the marriage falls apart.

A marriage is like an art,
Where no one is an artist,
I still remember it by heart,
I've definitely practiced.

Along the Salty Breeze

I live among the city birds
Far from my dear Norway,
Far from the rocks and fjords,
Far in the past and far away.

My mother heard the click,
Too late, no time to flee…
I was a little chick,
They captured me.

I crave the snowy storm,
I want the bitter freeze,
My freedom is so warm
Along the salty breeze.

Sunshine under my wings,
Over the cliffs of fiords,
I miss the songs of winds,
Sung by the downy birds.

I am too weak today,
Too old to sing or even fly,
Too old to get away,
My tears won't ever dry.

It is an idea people push,
A bird in the hand
Is worth two in the bush.

I am forever damned.

Obsession with Mortality

We're irrational when kindness
Lands on our weary shoulders,
When precious stones become
Cruel bone-crushing boulders,
Destroying every postulate
Of our moral guidance.
Leading into murky labyrinths
Of bottomless despair.
When the set of steps into Hell
Still widens,
But the old guardrails don't need
Repair.

While under a godsent overcast,
Under a dazzling quilt of mystery,
Our virtuous shortsighted hearts
Pledge slaughter of the arts.
Over a skeleton of times,
Over a dustbin of my past,
Over a garbage can of history,
We rush to solve all other crimes.

Our obsession with mortality
Won't carry modern trends.
I walk above pedestrian banality
Across the bridge to common sense.
I'll cross the Sea of Galilee;
I'll walk on water if I must,
But no one notices otherness in me
As said the Bible choking in the dust.

Nobody follows me.
Doors swing wide-open;
The end of time has spoken,
Death comes into my room.

Paul count Zeppelin R.I.P.
Was chiseled on my tomb.

Ambiguities

The birds won't sing
Without flowers in our gardens,
The bells won't ring
For our souls without pardons.

I never knew what is too much,
I never learned what is enough
In our mindless fighting.
I'm left behind by peers,
Who overlooked stop signs
While I enjoyed my happy years,
While I preferred a softer touch,
While I could madly fall in love
Between my constant writing,
Between my convoluted lines.

My conscience took a shower,
Then channeled my delusions
Into the bathtub's drain.
It is my liberating hour,
Without any wishful conclusions
Brewing in my still gullible
But rather piercing brain.

These days, I'm immune
To the slingshots and arrows
Of my dear foes and nasty friends
Who fight like hungry sparrows,
Digging in odds and ends.

I write it for the jockeys, not the horses;
I write it for the captains, not the ships;
I write it for the sinners in my home;
A burning bridge across my verses
Brings sparks into my final scripts
About ambiguities of the eternal Dome.

I'm not a part of the collective mind,
I'm not a part of any rebel crowd,
My death certificate is signed
By someone buried in that shroud.

Farewell to Happiness

Farewell to happiness,
The fee is awfully high,
I'm leaving you, unless
You kindly tell me why
We sin and we confess,
We laugh before we cry.

I silently endure
My sweet 'n sour pain;
I'm trying to be sure
It wasn't all in vain.

No effort is too big;
No effort is too small;
I'm not a petty prig;
I'm just against the wall.

My heart and every limb,
My soul and mind are sore;
Don't fill my patience to the rim,
I cannot take it anymore.

Is love still there or loath
In either or in both?
Farewell my happiness,
I'm leaving you, unless…

Farewell, Accordion

My worn accordion,
Still breathing "Hohner"
Is ready to retire,
Just like an aimless drone,
A bird without wings,
A moody, grumpy, loner,
An angel of desire,
A bard of sunny springs.

The day is crisp and dry,
But begging for some rain,
That could allow a chance
For this antagonistic sky
To cure my never-ending pain,
Brought by a nostalgic trance.

It's hard to say goodbye,
So long, a tired masterpiece,
Farewell, my old accordion,
You're too old to learn to fly,
Just rest in peace,
For life goes on.

Adorned with a Fruitless Glitz

Back to the glamour of my cradle,
I'm back to wave my last goodbye,
To pawn my birthright's silver ladle,
To find a softer grave to lie.

I wish to rest in peace
With my ancestors,
No monuments, no speeches, please,
Just a few exes with their new jesters.

I didn't write my memoirs;
They crawled straight out of Hell,
Out of wounds and wars,
Out of the fights in smoky bars,
Out of road motels with whores,
Out of a brutal horseless carousel.

The clay legged grandeur of my youth
Is wrapped in the darkest lies of truth.

My past was resting on the stage.
It's a lifetime shattered to the bits
Of poetry on every tattered page,
Nobly adorned with a fruitless glitz.

Farewell, My Strife

A house of cards,
Asylum for my whims,
Watched by the guards
Like in the horror films.

It is a tragic comedy
Of laughs and tears,
It is a quest to remedy
My vaudeville of fears.

I threw away my blindfold,
Then burned the bridge,
And to escape the hold,
I soared above the ridge.

A magic bird in hand,
Farewell, my strife,
Is it a pungent end
Or a first day of life?

Is life a futile golden cage?
Is it a mirror of grotesque?
Am I an actor on the stage
Of a miraculous burlesque?

As Uninvited Guests

The moment we're born,
We heave a sigh of great relief,
It is the end of our meatless diet.
We ask the doc for a piece beef;
He brings a basket of popcorn
And barks, "Shut up, be quiet.
There's no place for you to hide,
Get ready for a lifelong ride!"

God is away, the devil never fails,
We start our lifetime quests
Without guardrails
Or a parachute.
As uninvited guests
We pick the low-hanging fruit.

Nobody cares, nobody raves,
Nobody buys or reads our books,
While we're rocking on the waves,
The choosy fish avoid our hooks.

Life lets us swagger calmly,
Within a noisy crowd
Of gullible and giggly girls.
We hope they reckon fondly,
The days we ploughed
A football field of lovely pearls.

Sand castles fall into the sea,
We lose our thoughtless bets,
Life doesn't pledge or guarantee
That only fish come into our nets.

He Finally May Touch his Stars

He watched and painted from afar
A wonderful romancing;
The courteous moon was dancing
With a lonesome star.

Magnetic glory of the starry night,
Welcoming heaven for Van Gogh,
The paisley of the sky was bright,
Cozy and warm like a woven throw.

The red-hot vineyards,
The lemon-yellow sun,
The loyal purple shadows-guards
Couldn't protect him from his gun.

Redheaded Vincent,
Ill, poor and innocent,
Died in the labyrinth of farce,
He finally may touch his stars.

Greece

Banalities of progress,
Vulgarities of money,
Zeus' careless promise
Sunk in the sea of honey.

We relish our dawn in Greece,
The pinnacle of ancient worlds,
A sleeping giant in the breeze,
Clothed in wise Homer's words.

The Doric bastion of fading hopes,
Ionic elegance and grace of fate,
Corinthian columns on the slopes
Kept us alive before it was too late.

The cradle of civilization,
The holy grail of paradise,
A self-complacent nation,
An angel of divine demise.

Eternity for Writers

Nine lives for cats,
Eternity for writers
Killed in the staged combats
Then buried as overnighters.

A woman won't forget;
A man cannot forgive,
Life is a gambling bet:
Some win, some grieve.

My days are hacked
By many tearful goodbyes;
My nights are whacked
By playing games of dice.

I'd like to go back
To change my past
And run the longest track
Along the visions passed.

I've had enough
Of where I've been.
I've had enough
Of what I've missed.
I've had enough
Of what I've seen.
I never had enough
Of whom I kissed.

I'm a thirsty sheep, ram-led,
Inching towards the healing well,
But see the angels wearing red.
I guess it is too late; I am in Hell.

I scream, "My Lord, I am a poet!"
He quietly replies, "I know it."

Enlightened Failure

A bunch of psychedelic strangers
Holds signs: "Make Love, Not War".
They long and march for peace,
They fight, but only war arranges
Their fallen shadows on the floor
As if it is their destiny's caprice.

Numb silence shuts the door.
A spoken word is just a lie;
They make both love and war
And hear their mothers' cry.

Affairs erased their fear,
Love wore a velvet glove.
They dreamed of being here;
They wanted to be slaves of love.

They tried to balance loss and gain,
Their intentions overlapped.
They ran towards the end of pain;
Their wounds were never wrapped.

Stars fell on their hot heads,
Smiles cheered their faces,
They lived like jolly newlyweds,
Caged in their own embraces.

Enlightened failure of eternal glory
Depends on where I end this story.
Delusions of the future are in hands
Of those who paid the marching bands.

He Slowly Drags his Cart

He knows years of sorrows;
He knows tears of gratitude,
The fears of cold tomorrows,
The quiet cheers of solitude.

He walks lean like a fork;
He calmly drags his cart,
A sad and wingless stork
Carrying the guilt of ours:
A walk of a broken heart,
A funeral without flowers.

There is no place to hide
The stories of a street.
Dark shadow of his dog
Walks by his side
And jumps like a bullfrog
To catch his yummy treat.

Life is a relay's final leg.
Like a goat-legged faun,
He has to play and fight;
He has to bow and beg.
Like a graceful old swan,
Who fades into the night.

A homeless ragged man,
Well charred and seared
With a wine-colored face,
He took my five then ran
And quickly disappeared
Into the downtown maze.

A man who needs to rest,
A gullible, unrealistic child,
He wished us all the best
And strolled into the wild.

Four Silhouettes of Horses

Four silhouettes of horses
Loom in the dusty haze,
While a few ugly corpses
Mumble "Amazing Grace".

Late in the foggy morning
Before the high noon sun,
I heard the horses' roar,
Better-than-ever warning,
I fetched my old shotgun
And vainly locked the door.

Four riders show their valor
And float above the ground.
I'm horrified by every color
Of uninvited Merry-go-round.

Winds tore the nightly veil
Under the lightning's crack,
The last horse is quite pale,
Another's wrapped in black,
The white is perilously sad;
The one I really fear is red.

The most unwelcomed ghosts
From graveyards of nightmares
Attacked the sybaritic hosts
Of our self-indulging fairytales.

Daylights surrendered
To violent predictions,
To vigilantly feathered
Burdens and afflictions

We reaped what we have sown.
Generous angels passed us by,
Even tomorrow is unknown,
There's no time to say goodbye.

Four silhouettes of horses
Gallop between our corpses…

A Mirror

After a square-dancing stomp,
I brought a mirror to the face
Of our never-ending boredom.
It showed the abandoned swamp
That rests in peace of whoredom,
Entirely wrapped in spiders' lace.

The days of sadness
And annoying longing,
The nights of madness
And not belonging
To a band of brothers
That daily flies and sings.
I burned in war my wings.
The dead don't die again,
They walk from nothing
To nowhere.
Death is a deadened brain;
Death is a life no one can bear.
My soul tiptoes on cobblestones
Across our lackluster quiet town,
Only my body tearfully mourns
The sun that had to drown.

The sun sunk into its own sunset,
I cast no shadows anymore.
The crescent is too sleepy yet,
Rain knocks like the drums of war.

I never follow life
Through every open door,
Those who prevail in every strife
May lose the whole damn war.
Life is a whore. She drops a dress

Like autumn sheds its leaves.
I'm happy with much less;
I live among the praying thieves.
Ideas rarely ripen in their minds,
They stay half-baked quite long.
I hope to see among my finds,
The end of my unfinished song.

Anguish

What is the real end?
Life, death, or birth?
Old habits or a trend?
The sky? The earth?
My legacy's dustbins?
Baskets of wins and losses?
Tombs with the stars 'n crosses?
A few new legends of my sins?

I never knew the love of parents,
And their caressing hands;
I don't remember any presents,
Instead, I see a scorching glance.
I waited at the end of every queue
To justify and flaunt my genius IQ.

With nobody around,
I know what I loathe;
I'm forever purgatory bound;
I hate my Hippocratic oath.
My world is willfully obscure,
I write my verse in fits and starts,
I can no longer cure
These broken hearts
Or badly injured souls.
I amble in the dark without goals.

Winter arrived; it is too cold,
It is a decent time to fold;
The end is a stone's throw away,
It is too late to change my fate;
I am ill. Where is that stairway?
Where is that gate?

Ode to Love

I'll dress my bride in hugs and kisses.
I'll turn her joyful teardrop into a pearl.
She is so gorgeous and delicious,
I can't imagine any other girl.

The saints are watching from above,
The birds are singing with obsession,
White bells of lilies ring our tune of love
As innocently sensitive as a confession.

White little birch, please, be my bride;
Don't read a textbook's dated pages,
Let's find our promised land. I'll guide.
We'll love and wander through the ages.

Four Apocalyptic Horses

My four apocalyptic horses,
The food, the wine,
The travel morsels,
And friends of mine.

I'm happy and don't worry;
Apocalypse is not the end.
It's our never-ending glory;
It's just a day we all ascend.

I utterly enjoy the daily flow,
Life is a masked death row.
Life is a word nobody knows,
It's an enigma of tomorrows.
The truths and bluffs,
The failures of the arts,
The tragedies of loves,
And sighs of broken hearts.

I try to drop my nightly fears,
Their cruelty is fed by tears,
I never turn the other cheek,
I'm only tough amid the weak.

Axiomatic truths that never fail
Are white, red, dark and pale.
My four apocalyptic horses:
Great food, great wine,
Great travel morsels,
And friends of mine.

No One Hears the Cries

Our memories are warm
Under the coat of snow,
Only the fearless storm
Pulls off this cozy throw.

The darkness badly wants
To use its merciless knife,
Yet sunset bravely flaunts
A flare of our lackluster life.

The drums of latest wars
Still chill our blood in veins.
We fight on foreign shores
Whether it shines or rains.

Pain shut the doors
Of lands and skies,
Of woods and fields,
Of homes and stores,
Thus, no one hears the cries
Of our battles' fruitless yields.

I Hate this Rain

There are no don'ts and dos,
Only the innocence of souls;
I never tracked taboos,
But learned the brawls.

I can no longer run: I stroll,
The tears run from my eyes,
Rain's pouring from the skies
Over my brittle naked soul.

The clouds of the quiet skies
Caress the trees and flowers,
The rainbows bend and rise
After the daily showers.

I cannot stop this rain
Of bitter unrelenting tears;
I live and dream in vain
Under a waterfall of years.

I hate this endless rain;
I am alone and bored.
It's like a passing train
Had cut a mother's cord.

Like an abandoned boat
I am docked and chained;
Life's playing sink-or-float,
I am playing fight-or-faint.

I Borrowed Glee

A cozy half-baked dream
Is like equality for the unequal;
Some laugh, some scream,
The Heavens have no sequel.

I lost myself, I am racked
In our perfect paradigm,
The decks are stacked
By greedy hands of time.

I borrowed glee
Just for a day or two,
I hope it lets me flee
And soar into the blue.

The lights are fading,
I make my slouched stroll,
I am passionately waiting;
I am a teacher grading
God's efforts in creating
Some purpose for my soul.

These days I am reflected
Upside-down in the puddles,
I wonder if I'll be resurrected
As rainbows in their bubbles
Or in the fountains of glee,
Away from daily troubles.

I Ceased the Rain

I hate it when someone
Stabs me in the back,
I hate it when someone
Shoots me in the head,
I'm a martyr, I'm a rack,
Don't cry, I'm not dead.

Another angel fell,
The sky was mute,
I sense a gory spell,
And reap a sour fruit.

A fresco on the ceiling;
A fragile bliss of being;
Elusive beams of light
Above the devil's head;
A murky petrifying sight
Of our wilted daily bread.

I saw a sinful dawn,
I saw a dark sunset,
I heard a singing swan.
I swiftly placed my bet,
And dashed away
Into my yesterday.

Above the wall of sorrows
I found remedies for pain,
I failed to see tomorrows,
At last, I ceased the rain.

I had to Bite the Bullet

A face adorned with braids,
A scent of lilac slowly fades,
I met a girl, I held her hand,
I knew, she was a godsend...

I fought the tide of muggy fear,
I was afraid to lose what's dear.

I didn't want the world to stop,
I dreamed about seeing dawn,
A naughty rooster woke me up,
She was already gone...

She was the sweetest dream;
She was the worst nightmare.
She vanished in my scream,
The echo hid our short affair.

My destiny is sealed,
I never tried to fool it,
I loved and lived,
I had to bite the bullet.

I Bet She Had Two Wings

I met a gorgeous girl,
I bet she had two wings
Behind her back,
My head began to swirl,
I tried to pull the strings;
It was an offbeat track.

I am a foreigner, a stranger,
It was in Paris, at midnight.
I knew she would be my angel;
A darkness brought the light.

I gently kissed her hand,
A custom in her distant land;
I saw a shadow of her smile,
I was encouraged for a while.

I stopped a checkered car,
Though I could stop a train,
Perhaps I went too far,
But I was born insane.

She led me to a nice hotel,
I rang a seen-it-all doorbell;
Inside, she let me lift her
As in the olden movie reels,
My heart ran swifter
Than the taxi wheels.

Another French affair;
Another happy night,
Another rendezvous,
I said, "Mon petit chou",
And saw a happy glare.
It was the morning light.

Farewell, she shed a tear;
I visit Paris every year.

House of Cards

House of cards,
Familiar door,
Few failed whims,
Few broken hearts
Bleed on the floor
As in the horror films.

My endless grief,
My deepest sorrow;
My heart's belief,
There is a tomorrow.

There is new dawn:
The girls of Avignon,
Parisian Eiffel tower,
The mustard of Dijon,
Our daily happy hour.
Mozart, Shakespeare,
Delusions of King Lear
Remain after we've gone.

I hear our fat lady sings,
I see the angel's wings;
I watch the birth
Of bliss on Earth,
And cupids with their darts
Aiming at our eager hearts.

I Begged the Hurricane

Twenty-one grams of lead,
Twenty-one grams of wrath,
It is a bullet in my father's head,
It is a weight of our lives,
It is a shower of the falling knives
Into the heart of this bloodbath.
Into the glory of Euclidian geometry
For scientists and fools,
Into the blind oblivion optometry
Of detrimental Sunday schools.

My prayers won't be answered,
I don't believe they were received
By Lucifer or by the other gods,
Unreasonably once alienated.
Even the heavens were deceived
By silence of the lightning rods.

I begged the hurricane
To shred the clouds
And let the strings of rain
Send far away my doubts.

I climbed St. Peter's dome,
The splendor of a Holy writ,
Where sinners feel at home,
Enfolded in their caustic wit.

I crossed the continents and seas,
Ignoring knowledge of a maven,
In the pursuit of a Golden Fleece,
My odyssey came near safe haven.

I begged the hurricane
To bring the strings of rain.

Life isn't Idle with the Bitters

My pillow has no cooler side,
I watch my silent dreams
Next to my imaginary bride
While a TV set calmly gleams.

Life isn't idle with the bitters,
Sweet honey hurts my teeth,
I'm bored with the eerie fritters,
I want to see her bridal wreath.

I watch old movies every night;
My ecstasy arrives in black and white.
The dialogues are carved from pearls,
While Gable charms the Ziegfeld girls.

John Wayne rides a clever horse,
Flaunts shotguns or a brutal force.
Chivalrous Fred Astaire in a tuxedo,
And stud Weissmuller in his Speedo.

Alfred Hitchcock with vicious birds
And Casablanca's charismatic nerds,
Bacall and Bergman rule the nights,
Sinatra sings but Burt Lancaster fights.

My shadow doesn't follow me;
I'm petrified and breathe ozone.
The moon hangs on a naked tree
And lures me to the Twilight Zone.

I watch old movies every night,
I see my life in black and white.

Orgasms of History Were Faked

The history left us behind;
The laurels of a steamy glory
Didn't caress our tired heads.
We search, we have to find
Those who say: "Don't worry,
We shall exonerate your debts."

We break, at least, two eggs
To make our morning omelets;
Our bad ideas have two legs,
But march the road of regrets.

Those poets, artists, thinkers,
Who marched ahead of times,
Who tried to iron ugly wrinkles
Of punishments without crimes,
Paved our road straight to Hell.
They tutored us to soar. We fell.

Was it the dystopian ta le
About a courageous angel
Who is still christened fallen;
Or just the truth without a veil,
Or just a sovereign stranger,
Whose vanity was swollen.

Unhappy happy years,
Selective anecdotes of lies
Fall on the idle or deaf ears
And tease our blinded eyes.

Nostalgia is just a potent fertilizer
For our bouncing depressions;
It is a bag of futile pills from Pfizer,
The root of our fake confessions.

Half-baked conclusions
Corrupt or freeze our times;
The eerie mysteries are baked
With unachievable illusions
And wobbly paradigms.
Orgasms of history were faked.

My Epitaph

It's just a question I may ask,
"Is my retirement a dread,
Or just an unsteady truce
Between my head
That is already in the noose,
And the eternal loneliness
Wearing a happy mask,
Of courage under stress?"

We live like books that dwell
Between their covers
And never leave the shelves;
Our imagination never travels-
We're in love with ourselves.

The merciless bottom-lines
Of our lackluster lives
Are never sharpened knives
That lost their sparkly shines.

We wander in the desert
Of our solitude
Under the scorching sun,
Or sail across the icy waters
Of yet another friendless sea.

I'm too, not ready for the grave-
I wouldn't pawn my soul to God.
Death has to see that I'm brave,
When aims her lightning rod.

The mourners still laugh,
When read my epitaph:
"First to arrive,
The last to leave.
First in a daily strive,
The last to grieve."

Epitaph

There are no prisons and no walls
Dividing paradise and our souls,
Only the monotony of an eternal hum
Only a cacophony of urban sounds,
Only a silent singing for the numb,
Only the gaudy barking of the hounds.

My life consists of terminal addictions
To love, food, wine and loyal friends.
I do my best creating daily fictions
Until reality and hope connect at ends.

Sometimes, nostalgia can stroll
And pass the frosty window of my soul,
It's like the innocently naughty girls,
These unattainable and luteous pearls.

I guess, this imaginary action
As Newton's law vaguely states,
Didn't create an opposite reaction,
My past and I are laughing mates.

My days abruptly dwindle down
To the most precious few.
Sometimes, I'm acting as a clown,
Sometimes, I'm praying in a pew.

Yours, Paul
The same as ever.
P.S. I had it all,
But not forever.

I Hover in My Dreams

I am resting on the wind,
An old, dilapidated eagle,
Even my wings are trimmed,
I am just big, but never regal.

My beak is stretched
In agony of silent screams,
I cannot kill or fetch,
I hover only in my dreams.

I live without measures,
I write without rhymes,
I lost my treasures,
I failed the test of time.

My hopes don't climb,
My thoughts don't fly,
I hear the midnight chime,
You hear my last goodbye.

Epilogue

My writing is my passion and commitment as if I am always fighting for the one and only pigment I need to paint my life or lose in this tough strife.

Acknowledgements

I am a lucky guy having so many friends
who have read my poems and gave me
the most valuable recommendations.

I am endlessly obliged
To Judith Broadbent
for her devoted, enduring stewardship and
kindness, so generously shared with me;
For her skillful editing which gave me plenty
of space for my so-called "artistic freedoms".

To Anna Dikalova
for her constant trust in my
abilities, for her greatly inspiring suggestions,
and her doubtless expectations of success.

To Mary Anne Capeci
for her artistic wisdom,
Advices and a painting which she allowed
To use for a cover of this book.

To Nancy Blackwood and Lisa Baranets
for their "merciless corrections" of my verse.

Thank y'all as we, at times, say in Nashville.

Printed in the United States
By Bookmasters